Fast Track
Entrepreneur

Fast Track Entrepreneur

SUCCESS LEAVES FOOTPRINTS

PAUL OBERSCHNEIDER

FAST TRACK ENTREPRENEUR

Published by Harriman House Ltd
www.harriman-house.com

Visit pauloberschneider.com for more information.

ISBN 978-0-85719-680-4

TABLE OF CONTENTS

PREFACE

FEW PEOPLE CAN TELL YOU how to build a business worth hundreds of millions of dollars from nothing. But Paul Oberschneider can. And he'll do it in a way you've not likely heard before.

Highly successful serial entrepreneur, Start Up expert, business mentor, author and former Wall Street trader, Paul has achieved the kind of success that only a select few can boast.

Paul once told me that being a good leader is all about storytelling. If you can tell people your story in a way that makes them as passionate as you, they'll believe you. And it is his incredible story that guides this book.

Inside the Fast Track Entrepreneur, Paul introduces you to his Three Pillars of success—Mindset, Money, and Scaling—and explains how he used those essential tools and skills to build his empire.

Within this book, you won't find clichéd business advice, you won't read regurgitated and tired tips on how to manage your bottom line or how to take your business to the next level. Instead, you'll find honesty, humility and real practical advice that, for Paul, was more than once learned the hard way.

From a small-town childhood that was packed with both change and uncertainty, to successful Wall Street trader who lost it all and subsequently boarded a plane with his last $400 on a whim, Paul's story, and the lessons he took from it are more compelling and valuable than most. The tools of the trade he learned, and is now sharing with you are priceless.

Whether it's not listening to the experts, living with uncertainty and learning to accept fear and failure, finding those elusive blue-sky markets, building the best team, recognising your own limitations or simply arriving somewhere with the right mindset and just 'seeing what happens', each essential skill in this book is informed by Paul's life and success in business. It is, in essence, his story.

"Our lives are shaped by circumstances," he tells me. "Every entrepreneur has their own unique story and most who are successful have experiences in their past that drive them to succeed."

Growing up in idyllic rural Illinois during a period of great social, economic and cultural change Paul was exposed to an atmosphere where "positivity and excitement were in the air and it felt like anything was possible." At the same time, he had an unsettled home life due to the spectre of addiction that ran in his family.

Yet, it's precisely this set of circumstances that he believes prepared him so well for later life. "During my formative years, I was surrounded by this constant uncertainty while, at the same time, being exposed to immense change," he says. "Looking back, I think that really opened a lot of opportunities for me."

That ability to live with uncertainty is an essential survival skill in the competitive business jungle. For Paul, it was one honed in the cut-throat world of Wall Street—an experience he compares with "being thrown to the lions in the Colosseum every single day, and an environment full of risk, unpredictability and minute-by-minute change."

There can be few more competitive places than the Wall Street trading floor, and so it was for Paul who, while carving out a successful career, found the fact that there was no tangible measure of success difficult. Finding it hard to appreciate the value of money and enjoying the excesses that came with such a position, he spiralled into an addictive cycle that ultimately cost him his job.

This, however, was where life changed. And it's this moment that helps best identify the first of his Three Pillars: Mindset. It was a time in his life that he describes candidly as reaching the cliff edge and deciding whether to jump or not. "You need that birth by fire to really understand things," he adds.

"If you can survive something that terrible and make it out the other side, you'll always be able to do it again. Growing up around change, uncertainty and risk taught me how to think quickly, not to procrastinate and to be independent. It was the foundation for things I went on to do in the future that many wouldn't have ever taken on."

One of those things was to jump on a one-way plane bound for Estonia armed with his last $400 and no plan, no real idea of what he was going to do on arrival and no strategy.

"I was just there," he says. "I was ready, in the right mindset and prepared to just see what happened. I'm a firm believer that if you're in the right place then something will happen. All you have to do is be there, ready and have the right tool kit to enable you to succeed."

It worked. In a little over 18 years Paul established one of Central and Eastern Europe's largest real-estate businesses, helped start a bank, mortgage companies and five-star hotels and oversaw a portfolio of companies that was valued at more than $200million. All this, and he didn't even speak the language.

Admittedly, it's a bold approach, but it's one that's qualified by the many other skills Paul has learned, and which he lays out in his Three Pillars. Among those is having faith in—and understanding—just what you can achieve. As he says in Chapter 8 of his arrival in Estonia "I was alone, and yet I knew I was in the right place.

"To reach the point where you can truly be driven by circumstance you have to know where you came from, what you believe in and enjoy, what you are passionate about and what drives you."

It's a concept Paul calls 'where are you now?' and one that he elaborates on in these pages. Knowing oneself and being able to truly articulate and show those passions, strengths and desires is something that is a key part of Paul's mentoring work.

"Many people never take the time to know what they're really good at," he adds. "It's challenging, it's introspective but if you find it you'll be very fortunate. The best way to do it, though, is to not think too much about it. As I did, get out there and just show up; you'll intuitively discover what you're meant to do."

Of course, there is more to being a successful entrepreneur than having the right mindset, as Paul discovered on arrival in Estonia. After all, how does a guy that doesn't know anyone and doesn't understand the local language make $200million?

He does it by knowing his own strengths and limitations, and by building a strong team. It's a concept he elaborates in further in his third pillar, named Scaling.

"Build that team from day one," he notes. "Am I a hotelier? Am I a developer or banker? I'm none of those things, but I work well with people so in some respects I am all of those things at once."

For Paul, of course, the necessity of building that team was obvious—he needed people to be able to conduct business in their native language. Yet, the essence of what went into that team is the same for every entrepreneur: finding those skills you don't have in order to complement your leadership.

"Don't think you can be the expert," he reflects. "As an entrepreneur, you're a control freak, but doing everything doesn't allow your business to grow. I had to hire people because I couldn't do it myself and, because I was able to build that team and delegate efficiently, I was able to grow ten times faster than my competitors."

And it is here that we come full circle to the idea of storytelling. According to Paul, pulling that team together can only come from telling your story. How do you convince people to share your idea, to be part of something that everyone can believe in? By sharing a vision or—in the case of this book—a journey.

There is much more to Paul's story than I've managed to tell. But you'll find it interweaved in every essential skill in this book. It is in equal parts inspiring, informative and entertaining, and one that looks at the world of entrepreneurship with refreshing honesty.

But perhaps most importantly, it is one that makes you realise anything is possible. As Paul says, "If I can do it, why can't you?".

—Matthew High is an experienced freelance editor and features writer. He has been an editor and journalist for a number of magazine titles including Start Up entrepreneur magazine, and Aspire; RR, the official global lifestyle magazine for Rolls-Royce Motor Cars.

THE BASICS

FAST-TRACKING PRINCIPLES lie at the heart of every business success these days. As a Fast Track entrepreneur, you will need to follow certain crucial business rules in order to compete. You will need to understand what works and what doesn't at key critical moments, and if it doesn't work then move on. It is a competitive jungle, and knowing these rules will determine your survival.

By mastering each of the Fast Track rules, you will be equipped for any business encounter. At the end of this book you will have learned tools that will help you to build a successful business quickly and also help you with the following essential skills:

— Ability to find business opportunities
— Ability to create a business idea
— Ability to structure a team around you
— Ability to find the funding you need
— Ability to create the right brand
— Ability to build baskets of revenue streams

INTRODUCTION

Fast is Better Than Slow

FIRST OF ALL, DON'T PANIC. Sometimes it feels like you are grasping at straws. One minute you think you know the answer, the next minute you don't. But you must act. You must do something. There is information overload, and then there is the possibility of failure. You feel stuck; afraid to take that leap.

Welcome to the jungle, you are a Start Up.

Every entrepreneur has these moments of self-doubt and fear. It's part of the job. This is your baby, you are the CEO and the buck stops with you—but do you have what it takes? Sadly, most people don't. You need to move quickly.

In today's fast-paced world, where technology has shrunk the time factor by a zillion, you need to stay ahead of the curve. You need to be adaptive and change, and have the tools to do so. What used to take ten years now takes six months—and there is often someone looking to do it faster—so you need to think and act quickly.

Most of the time, you'll be in survival mode, even when things are going swimmingly, because sands shift and your competition is right behind you. So, you need to stay focused. And you need a plan. You can't let your family or the people who support you down. It's a lot of weight to carry, so who can you ask for help? Who knows the answers that can guide you? What I've learned is that success leaves footprints and you don't need to reinvent anything.

You can't do it all on your own so you will need to build and share a story and a vision with people. You will have to convince funders and bankers to support you, put everyone in the right place at the right time, and then learn to delegate and trust. When it all goes wrong, everyone will look to you for answers and it is down to you to regroup and start again.

Okay—so you get all that, but like I asked before, who can help you? Remember, I told you success leaves footprints…

I'm Paul Oberschneider. A successful Fast Track Entrepreneur and man of the competitive business jungle. My own business journey started with little more than $400 and an idea, but in emerging markets and frontier countries where I didn't even speak the language, I managed to build on that idea to create a succession of profitable companies to the tune of $200 million.

Success leaves footprints, and I've been on your journey already. As a successful entrepreneur and CEO, I've got scars and bruises to show for it! There's no smoke, no mirrors—I'm just here to share the plain truth of what works and what doesn't in the competitive jungle of Start Ups.

I'm sure you've seen the stats; the small business failure rate is going up and up each year, not down. Forty percent of businesses fail in their first year, and more than 80% within the first five years, and 94% inside ten years. What's left are the 6% who make it, and of those, only 10% will ever make more than $1million in sales.

You need to know what you're up against, but you can do it and I can help. You see, if I did it, there is no reason why you can't do it, too.

You'll learn my Fast Track entrepreneur strategies, and I'll share fundamental tools you'll need to survive in the jungle. So, let's get started.

This book is laid out in three individual sections; Mindset, Money, and Scaling a business. These are broken down into chapters, each relating to a lesson, topped off with interviews of entrepreneurs like yourself who have tackled a problem and come out the other side. You can learn from people who have been there, faced the same problems as you and successfully found solutions, leaving you with a checklist of action points to take away. That way you can act quickly and Fast Track with the answers at your fingertips.

You're lucky. I wish I'd had something like this when I was starting out, as it would have made the journey so much easier! Good luck and let's go…

PART 1: MINDSET

WHAT IS MINDSET?

It's the way you see the world. It's what you think you are. Because you are what you think you are.

There's a great story of a man who finds an eagle egg by the side of the road. The man sees that the egg has fallen from the high branches of a tall tree, so he picks it up, takes it home and rests it in his chicken coop. The egg hatches and the eagle is born.

But the eagle is raised by chickens and it learns to cluck. It pecks at the ground and flaps around the yard without every really getting off the ground. It has no idea it is an eagle.

One day it sees another eagle soaring above. The chickens tell him the bird is an eagle, the king of all birds. But they are just lowly chickens. Sadly, the eagle lives and dies a chicken.

Because he thought he was a chicken.

You may need to change your thinking. You need to know what you want and adjust your mind to think that way. Because at the end of the day, we are what we think we are, and the way you think can either be your greatest asset or your worst enemy.

If we are going to be great, to survive in a competitive world we need our heads on straight. It's all about having the right mindset to follow your dreams.

FAST TRACK RULE 1

Understanding Failure and Why Failure is Good

BILL GATES SAYS: "Success is a lousy teacher. It seduces the smartest people into thinking they can't lose."

On top of the many challenges of starting a business, you need to know when you are wrong, and when it is time to fold. Sometimes you have to surrender first in order to win later. I learned that a long time ago. There was a guy I knew and he always used to tell me "surrender to win" and I never really understood. Now I do. Know when you're wrong, admit where you are and let it go. Don't fight in the jungle. It's way too dangerous!

Just know that of all the businesses that are started, more than 40% fail in the first year, and up to 94% fail in the next ten years. What's left over make it. So you're not alone if things go wrong—in fact, you're among very illustrious company.

As an entrepreneur, you're going to try many things and have lot of ideas. Most of them will be rubbish and won't work. You'll fail a dozen times and make all kinds of mistakes. But don't be discouraged, it's how you handle mistakes that counts. Know they are inevitable, know they are okay to make and know that they will teach you so you don't make them again. They are part of the process, so embrace mistakes and failure. Don't let them get you down or make you embarrassed.

If you had $100 to invest, and you minimised each loss to only ten dollars, you could trade ten times before losing it all. Ten tries is a lot. Chances are that if you were disciplined enough to do that, eventually you would be right, and the winners would make you enough money to cover your losses. And if you pyramid on your winners and add to them as they grow, you could even multiply your gains. As a Fast Track Entrepreneur, you need to know when to cut bait.

Of course, losing takes its toll, both emotionally and financially, so it's better to stop early, regroup and start again rather than endure a lingering business death. Admitting insolvency and facing family and friends after a failure is a hard thing to do and, for a while, might make it all seem worse. But things will eventually improve, and it is better to get it over with.

Going to the bank and borrowing more money is rarely the answer. Asking your family to back you even more certainly isn't, either. Just stop if it's not working, regroup and start again. Your original business idea might have been a good one, but if you're now under a weight of debt because you executed it poorly or failed for any reason, there is really no better way forward than to cut your losses and close down the business.

People become attached to their businesses, so they hold on and continue to throw good money after a bad idea. They had a reason for starting their business in the first place, and they struggle to admit that they were wrong. They always think their losses will turn around, but they usually don't. Most investors and new business owners do exactly the opposite of what they should do. They hope, and it is the hope that kills us. If that's where you are, stop and then run for the hills because it's going to get ugly.

It never gets better, only worse. So, don't be attached to any one thing. By the way, that includes negative people or bad relationships. If it's not working, start again. Life's too short to be in chronic pain or fear. Don't struggle with the temptation to doggedly try over and over again, expecting a different result. Don't remain wedded to an idea that hasn't worked. Being stubborn doesn't make you smart.

Also, when you hit the wall of failure, it's better for everyone to know what's really going on. That means backers, bankers and anyone else who is important. This builds trust, and it's the right thing to do. It's not a failure to be wrong and shut down your idea or business. The only failure is not getting out when you should. Everyone makes mistakes and they will understand as long as you stop it early enough.

If your business isn't making money—if you constantly need to subsidise it with more funding—don't fool yourself, your investors or your bankers into thinking it will come around. Be brave and honest. There's no harm in being wrong and failing. If it's not working now, chances are it won't ever work. In life and in business, just get the hell out before the failure becomes spectacular. One failure is not the end of your entrepreneurial ambitions, but failing to learn will be.

It's better to be persistent than dogged. Being persistent means if your business idea isn't working, you don't give up, but you do change the way you're doing things and try again. Doggedness means doing the same thing over and over and expecting the results to be different. Many people get these two attitudes confused. Don't let it be you!

FOOTPRINT 1

UNDERSTANDING WHY FAILURE IS GOOD
SAM JONES, CO-FOUNDER & MD TUNAFISH MEDIA

Biography

Sam Jones is the Managing Director of Tunafish Media, a content marketing and media production agency he co-founded (alongside Richard Brooks & James McDonald) in 2011 at the age of 22.

Despite having no formal business training, Jones has led Tunafish into one of the UK's most critically acclaimed creative agencies winning over 30 major industry awards for their work. Jones has also been named 'Entrepreneur', 'Media Entrepreneur' and 'Communications Professional' of the year by the JCI, EN Magazine and DIB respectively and was named as one of Insider Magazine's 42 under 42; a list of business people to watch under the age of 42.

In your opinion, why is failure good?

I've learnt a lot more from failure than I have success. I think failure is healthy and is needed to truly grow. As long as you can learn from it, and be aware of falling into similar traps in the future, that increase in knowledge can only be a good thing.

What big failure do you think was helpful or responsible to your success?

When we started this business, we had in our heads that it would be an overnight success and that just isn't how it works. We were young and there was definitely a level of naivety there and because of that, we made a lot of mistakes.

Those mistakes have been instrumental to our growth both as a business and individuals. I think the biggest mistake I made was chasing opportunities that were not really right for us and we wasted a lot of time and effort chasing down blind alleys. That's made me a lot more aware moving forward what is right for us and what isn't.

Today you're a successful entrepreneur, but if something went terribly wrong, do you think you could come back from that?

I do. If I'm honest, I would definitely take some time to dust myself over and get my thoughts together. I'd then spend some time finding a project that excites me before going again. Although it's important to bounce back, I feel it's equally as important not to rush in.

FAST TRACK RULE 2
Don't Listen to the Experts

EVER SINCE WE WERE AT SCHOOL, we have always been taught that there is a right way and a wrong way. We're told that some things can be done and that others can't. There are smart people and, of course, there are not-so-smart people.

None of us like to make mistakes, so what do we do? We ask for help and advice. We ask the experts. Experts are people who know more than we do. People that have that special badge of education and maybe a degree. Of course, they know better than we do. Why? Because they are the experts and have acronyms and letters on their business cards.

But it's wrong. Totally all wrong. Especially in today's world of fast-moving information and disruptive change.

Back in 1992, I was trying to raise two nickels for my property business in Eastern and Central Europe. These were all new emerging markets. The Berlin Wall had recently fallen and there was a curious interest in these new markets. I went to the experts for advice and looking for capital; I went to those who are the gatekeepers of capital.

First off, most of them had never even heard of some of the countries; mentioning names such as Czech Republic, Estonia, Latvia, Lithuania, Poland and Hungary drew blank stares. One expert even asked me if there wasn't a war going on (I assume he was thinking of the Balkans).

I recall sitting in a panelled office on Hanover Square in London talking to two real estate experts. They were from a large property company and looked pretty sharp in their pin-striped suits and pink shirts. They asked me lots of questions with terms I had never heard of before and I felt ridiculously stupid. Finally, in their wisdom, they told me these markets would never amount to anything; they were too small and shallow and investors would never be interested. There was too much risk. I walked out feeling pretty low.

Go figure. I guess years later I felt vindicated, in a similar way to Steve Jobs after his triumphant return and success at Apple. Not surprisingly, because over the following years I went on to build $200million worth of property in these markets and sold them to these exact same experts in 2008 before the crash. Just saying.

And the funny thing is that those two guys are still there doing their expert job. I met one of them this past year, and I asked him about some new markets I was interested in in Africa. This person is the head of the African department of his firm. He told me that these markets were done and then went on rattling about how they were unsafe, corrupt and investors would never go there. Guess what—I'm buying my plane ticket the first chance I get, because if he's selling then I'm buying.

Okay, back in Central and Eastern Europe in the early '90s I was early. It's not easy to be early but once you are there, and assuming you stay there, you will be firmly entrenched. Later, all the experts would come rushing in between 2004 and 2008 and by then of course, it was too late and they would get clobbered when the bubble popped.

As an entrepreneur, you need to be early and you need to see ahead before anyone else does. You need to see way ahead of the crowd to be successful.

So don't be fooled by the experts. They don't know. It's not their fault; they just travel the path of security and certainty. And if you're an entrepreneur with an idea, trying to change or save the world, and surviving in the competitive jungle, then you need to know right away that these experts will always be wrong. Always. You're too early and that's a good thing. But the answer you are looking for just isn't there from them.

You're going to have to go with your gut, your intuition. Because at the end of the day, that's what you're going to get paid for—your intuition. This is what makes you different to everyone else, and it is what will make you or break you. If not, you might as well put on a suit and a pink shirt and go to work each day at 8am on Hanover Square.

If all the great business leaders and entrepreneurs had listened to the experts, we wouldn't have many of the things we simply take for granted today. Go ahead and meet them and listen to them—collecting information is invaluable when it comes to making decisions, and they're great for getting the data you'll need to discuss with other experts. You'll learn their language and you'll get good at speaking it. You'll need to listen because at some stage you'll be fundraising and you'll need to have answers that they can understand. In fact, you'll probably be selling to them one day so you need to know what they look for.

But just remember, as you're walking out of a meeting feeling stupid, these people don't know any more than you do. If they did, they'd be playing polo or relaxing on their yachts. That's what you're going to do.

FOOTPRINT 2

DON'T LISTEN TO THE EXPERTS
PAUL GRIFFITHS, CEO & CO-FOUNDER BLOODSTONE SOLUTIONS

Biography

Paul Griffiths is the CEO at Bloodstone Solutions, a tech startup, mentor at Toucan Ventures, an eco-system that supports creative potential as a long-term partner through the tough startup phases by using a Mentor and Investor network. Paul is also an advisor at C4DR, a multi-city business development hub comprising a built-in international corporate foundry, a series of startup challenge programmes targeting key industry verticals, and an in-house 4IR think tank. Prior to this, he worked with serial entrepreneur Sir Stelios Haji-Ioannou on a whole range of businesses at various stages as well as holding numerous 'C' suite positions based around fintech and the sharing economy.

Can you give us an example at the beginning of your entrepreneurial journey where you were almost put off by an expert opinion?

A few years ago, I was working on a sharing economy project, trying to raise some capital to grow it. The sharing economy even now is still a fairly new concept, but at that time it was in its infancy and pre-Uber, so for most people it was an unknown quantity. I met a so-called expert and was explaining the business only to be told it was a terrible idea, all the reasons why it would not work and that I was wasting my time. This was a bombshell, especially from someone who I believed knew their stuff.

Why didn't you listen—or did you?

I spent a few hours considering what I had been told, and then concluded he just didn't understand it, but rather than say that, chose to rubbish my ideas. I was very lucky, within a few days I was contacted by a VC fund I had previously pitched to and they told me they were ready to invest and we went on to become one of their best investments.

Today when you listen to people, how do you assimilate that advice and move ahead?

I take all 'advice' with a pinch of salt. I listen to it, then I try to work out what qualifies that person to give that advice. Is it just an opinion? Do they have their own agenda? The problem with experts is that that they sell themselves based on their views— if yours does not match theirs, how can they understand?

FAST TRACK RULE 3
Look for the Unexplored Jungle
(The Blue Sky)

ENTREPRENEURS TODAY FACE a market that is more fast-paced than ever before, and with more than 600,000 new businesses starting in the US alone every year, it pays to look for markets with freedom to create.

Every year, business failure rates keep rising. Technology is making things happen faster and faster and it is disrupting old ways of doing things. More than 80% of all business Start Ups fail in the first five years. It's a bloody red hot competitive jungle out there. After ten years, only 6% are left standing, and of those businesses, only 10% will make more than $1million.

So, to level the field you need to stand out and be different

One day, I sat looking at a big world map on the desk in my office in Oxford. I flipped open the map at the page showing Africa and pointed at a spot. My finger landed on a lake in Ghana, specifically on Lake Bosumtwi. Near the lake stands a tropical city of 1.7million people called Kumasi. It's famous for its flowers and plants and has a high school, a university and a teaching hospital. For people who know the city, it's in decay. At least that's what Wikipedia said about it last time I looked.

With a little more browsing online, I quickly found out that if you happen to be an expat looking for a night out in Kumasi, you'll have your choice of pizza, Indian food or even an El Gaucho restaurant. Being a lover of Tex-Mex food, I was curious if you could get tacos or a burrito there. Nope. No Mexican burritos. So if you're aching for Mexican food in this 100-degree tropical city, you're going to be disappointed. You might have to go somewhere else.

It's what I like to call a blue-sky market. Like all opportunities in emerging markets, the window will close quickly. If I do the same research in a few years' time there may be a number of great Tex-Mex outlets competing for my custom, but for a while at least, an entrepreneur will have blue sky and be the only game in town. That makes all the difference before the wall of liquidity and banking comes rolling in.

Now, you might think the streets of Kumasi are the last place you would want to run a restaurant, but people are eating, and even in poor countries and cities, a meal out is often what people do for a celebration or just a social gathering as a distraction from everyday life. So why not Mexican food? There's no one else in the market, and it's certainly a big market.

When you're thinking about a business or sector to launch in, look for a market or opportunity where competition is lacking. Opening a quick service food business in one of London's hottest sectors means trying to muscle your way into a crowded market. There are thousands of guys doing the same thing. You're not going to solve anyone's problem by launching another fast food chain. Open a chain of hot dog stands instead!

Try to stand out and look for uncontested space or for blue sky. I look for that African market where little competition exists. Blue sky is a market or opportunity where you are free to create and explore before everyone else catches up. It's where there is little competition and pricing is still inelastic— in economics, this means demand doesn't fall regardless of a rise in price.

Hot markets always look promising and often seem easy to enter. I look at the crowdfunding market today, and yes, it's tempting. Yes, it's hot out there, and Internet entrepreneurship appears to be growing. Fast food is crazy. But no one is making any money because they are all competing for the same sites, and restaurant property rent is way above where it should be as a percentage of sales.

A hot market is both crowded and competitive. Remember, by the time the market is sizzling hot, the tide has already risen and taken people to the top. The trick is to create and explore before everyone else knows the territory.

Decide where you are and what's missing near you. What are people lacking? What can be improved? What's being done successfully elsewhere that can be twisted and adapted to work where you are? If you're alone, you'll either be rewarded almost immediately, or at least you'll find out how stupid your idea is pretty quickly. Neither are bad results.

F O O T P R I N T 3

LOOK FOR THE UNEXPLORED JUNGLE
JULIE CHOO, FOUNDER & CEO AT STRATABILITY

Biography

Julie Choo is the Founder of Stratability. Having come from an engineering background, Julie accelerated her career by using the latest technologies like AI and Big data to change and grow businesses. She has helped many organisations—especially in Fintech—to innovate, while fine-tuning their business models and operating models. Through the training and advisory services offered by Stratability, Julie and her team help others to build the 'Strategic Capabilities' they need to succeed in their businesses. Julie invented THE STRATEGY JOURNEY® framework, that provides five models to help businesses transform with agility, accountability and action (book out in 2018).

When you started your business, how much competition was there in your market space?

As the name suggests, Stratability stands for 'Strategic Capabilities' and that's what I set out to offer customers when I started the company in late 2015, while still a freelance consultant to large corporates and venture capital backed startups. At the time of starting my business, the market for consultants (and especially in Fintech in London) was already saturated. I knew I could offer a better service than most of my competitors, but they were bigger and had more marketing and sales resources than me, a one-person company. It was near impossible to stand out from the crowd and get noticed.

Can you tell us what made you different—and did that make it easier or harder?

I started to change the way I offered my services to customers and looked for different customers that were not served, but who still wanted what I had to offer, while being able to pay, too. I offered learning services through e-learning and classroom workshops, rather than consulting, and changed my message to 'help organizations and people to help themselves'. Through different networks and channels, I started to offer my services to markets like Australia and Singapore where people and organizations value education and learning more than in the UK, and hence were willing to pay more, too.

Do you still look for uncontested space today, or do you think you can create an uncontested market in a competitive market?

I actually teach how to carve out new markets, especially in a competitive environment, in my book. In the fintech space, you just need to look at the regulations that are coming in and changing all the time, and use these to your advantage. Closed markets can be disrupted.

FAST TRACK RULE 4
Be a Machine of Ideas

'WHERE DO I START?' I hear you wondering. Chances are, if you're like me, you'll have a hundred great ideas every day. Crazy or impractical ideas in your quest for a successful Start Up, maybe, but eventually the perfect idea will strike at just the right time. It won't be a eureka moment, the clouds won't part, but it will happen and suddenly you'll be swimming in it. You need to make sure you're open to the eureka moment and you're awake to act.

I think that ideas float around in space. We're all privy to them, but some of us are more awake than others. We need to be open-minded, always searching and asking questions and looking for opportunity. We're trying to survive and we need to be hunters.

Make a habit of brainstorming. Like I said, you'll probably have at least 20 ideas a day. 20 great ideas! They come and go. Ideas are perishable. They come in a blink of an eye, and they hit us without warning. A half-hour later, you've forgotten them.

Don't be surprised, but most of your ideas are great. They are yours so of course they're great! But they're probably impractical. One day, you may have an amazing idea about international money transfers, and the next day you might envision how to do stocktaking for a fast food chain. But if you're not in those sectors already, chances are it will be extremely difficult for you to get any traction without investing significant time and resources. That's not to say that it can't be done, but it's a longer shot. I can't be everything and there's only so much time in a day to learn (we'll come to this key important point later on), so I suggest you try and stay as close as you can to your comfort zone.

Bear in mind that the dots of ideas can be connected in ways you never would have imagined. Being in your comfort zone does not mean lack of creativity—far from it. You're using your knowledge base to expand your thinking. When all's said and done, it may look like a straight A to Z path, but actually you'll be jumping all over the map. Each of your seminal ideas will sneak up on you, slowly developing in their own magic way, until suddenly there's a confluence into one Big Idea. But you'll have travelled over some bumpy roads in the meantime.

Remember that the golden idea is almost always one that fits with your skills or what you've always dreamed of doing. Find that patch that you enjoy. What makes you happiest? What do you like doing? That's where you will find the right ideas. The worst thing is to do something because you think you have to or just because that's what others are doing.

But keep in mind ideas are universal. For every idea we have at any given moment, there will be someone else somewhere in the world having the same thought. It's really circumstances that determine who makes it work and who has the ability to move forward with that idea at that time. To a certain extent, luck is about being in the right place at the right time, as some people say, but really, it's the confluence of circumstances and being ready. So just show up each day and wait for that tap on the shoulder. One day you'll grab the right idea that fits the place you're at, and you won't even know it's coming.

When you find your winning formula, you're likely to be doing something you know about and have already been drawn to. If you start with one thing, it will eventually take you down the right path without you noticing. Chances are the business you want to start or are involved in right now is related to something you know about, or are passionate about, or have been thinking about for some time.

Consider your circumstances. Keep asking yourself "Where are you now?" Remember that steps towards your vision are a confluence of your ideas and your circumstances; one day you'll grab the right idea that fits the place you're at. Look at

Bill Gates. Why was he so successful compared with others? It was because Bill Gate's mother had the only computer lab in her school in America at the time. Bill had the advantage.

Look at your unique circumstances and what you're doing right now. You really can't get to point B if you don't know where A is. So, size it all up and have a look. And you don't need to know *how* to get to point B right away. You just need to have a grasp of the general direction, and then keep correcting your course as you go. Steve Jobs studied graphics and design; he didn't go into fast food. When you take strides toward your vision, you'll come to know your arena pretty well, and your business ideas will be a reflection of where YOU stand in that arena.

FOOTPRINT 4

BE A MACHINE OF IDEAS
RANI SAAD, FOUNDER & CEO IN THE WINDOW, INVESTOR

Biography

Rani has built and invested in ventures in the US, UK and elsewhere for more than 20 years. He has co-founded or co-built four technology startups in Silicon Valley, London and Los Angeles, in addition to a $120m emerging-markets VC fund. He also launched products globally and directed innovation acceleration in more than 70 countries at Microsoft, led venture formation at a leading behavioural design entity, and launched cutting-edge fintech platforms at a Fortune 500 bank. Rani also invests in leading-edge tech startups, serves as a judge in Stanford's Ignite programme for innovation and entrepreneurship, and advises startups, funds and organisations (which have included the World Bank) on early-stage innovation. Rani holds an MBA from Stanford and degrees in three engineering fields (master's in Intelligent Transportation Engineering and a bachelor's in Computer and Communications Engineering).

Ideas are a dime a dozen; how do you make sure your ideas are the right ones'?

I don't believe that a perfect idea exists. They all need iterative refinement, adaptation and, possibly, pivoting. The question is how to rank them. I do so on three primary dimensions: novelty, actionability and scalability. Assessing these dimensions is influenced by one's profile, context and resources. The ideas that score highest for me, I delve deeper on.

One of my favourite ways to delve deeper is with the

"five-why's". Asking why five times in succession helps uncover the underpinning drivers and assumptions. This not only gives a preliminary level of validation, but also sharpens my thinking around the opportunity and, indeed, may give rise to derivative ideas that could be even more profound and powerful. Once an idea crystallizes, it's important to plan and take some action—first steps—to give it life and start sculpting it, otherwise, it would likely perish. Framing the scope of action is important. A common challenge in scoping is finding your 'Goldilocks zone'; if too narrow, it won't offer room for creative exploration; if too broad, it's difficult to tackle and action.

What if you're working on an idea—and suddenly you realise there is someone already in the same space doing it the way you wanted—do you give up, or does that simply validate your idea?

Discovering someone is already taking action on an idea always presents a challenge. It, however, can also offer valuable learnings. If the other party is credible and gaining traction, it helps validate the idea. More importantly, if internalized constructively, this can guide us to refined differentiation and stronger positioning. Constraints breed creativity and innovation.

Competition moreover drives the whole space forward, accelerating scale and growth. It will, of course, produce casualties—but that's the game. Earlier entrants also serve a valuable role: they prime investors and educate customers on the opportunity, benefiting everyone in the space.

Tell us how your circumstances in early life gave you the unique ideas that were the foundation of your business.

I grew up in a highly volatile, very small developing country, where existential risk was omnipresent and opportunities were limited and dear. That developed a hunger for opportunities and a necessity for creative agility in unearthing them.

FAST TRACK RULE 5
Share Your Vision

YOU MAY BE PASSIONATE about your Start Up, but you can only make it great by inspiring your customers and team with a vision. Be a great storyteller and share your passion—make *your* thing *their* thing! Don't be afraid to have a big goal. Far more is possible than you've let yourself dream.

In order to inspire others, you need to conjure up something original, different, new, bigger or better. The sky's the limit. Remember Blue Sky?

Grab your notebook and sketch out a draft version of your goals. It may feel strange at this stage to be mapping out a fantasy, but the process of writing it all down starts to make your ideas more concrete. Remember that you are looking to stand out, find uncontested space and do something no one else is doing. You will need to craft that idea into a story. Writing and storytelling are powerful tools and key skills for anyone who wants to build a company. You are telling the story of the future success of your business, so make it exciting!

I'll give you an example of the power of writing. When I was applying to graduate business school, I had to write roughly ten essays per school. I applied to ten schools. That's a lot of essays. The questions were always nearly the same, such as "tell us your long-term plans for the future. How will you add value to society?" So, I wrote a lot and most of my answers were the same, so it was a repetitive process. I didn't know it but by writing down stuff over and over I forcing myself to think things through, and I was brainwashing my subconscious.

And what happened? All the things I wrote on those essays came true. It's amazing but that's what writing can do.

So, write and simplify. Write and tell your story so that you can explain it easily to others. Effectively sharing your dream with other people is critical to building the right team of employees, investors and consultants and, ultimately, to persuading customers to buy your service or product. By the laws of attraction, if you can get your passion across, others will share it. Write your idea out again, and this time add pictures to show how it looks in your head. This may feel silly at times, but it truly is important! Writing is action, so the plan will become stronger with every rewrite. And pictures take the idea from the visual part of your mind to the paper in a way that's stronger than words.

Let go and let it happen. Once you've started to write, it can lead to all kinds of things. When you finally manage to get it the way you want it on paper, your brain has gone through an amazing process. Time to sit back and see where it takes you...

Be flexible and keep revising your plan. When you write something down over and over, it gets clarified. You create a powerful tool to make your goals come true. But you will need to constantly revise as circumstances change. Listen to people's feedback and use it to improve what you already have.

FOOTPRINT 5

SHARE YOUR VISION
CLARA DURODIÉ, CEO COGNITIVE FINANCE GROUP

Biography

Clara Durodié is a business technologist with Board of Directors experience and an expert in applied artificial intelligence (AI) in finance. She has served in leadership roles in asset and wealth management in the UK, Switzerland and Luxembourg. Clara is the CEO of Cognitive Finance Group (CFG), a consultancy and investment company focused on applied AI in financial services firms for the correct adoption, selection and implementation of AI systems.

Clara works with Board of Directors, academia and AI startups at leading fintech accelerators. Her focus is risk management and business intelligence for profitability and growth. Clara is a member of the Chartered Institute for Securities and Investment (CISI) London UK, has a Certificate in Investment Management and holds a master's degree from the University of Oxford.

Do you consider writing an important part of being an entrepreneur?

Writing means putting the intention out. If it's clear in your mind, it's clear to the rest of the world. Clarity of mind is clarity of thinking. I always ask my team to visualize what they want to achieve every day, and write it down. This is one reason we have our morning meeting every day at 9am London time.

When you were starting and as you work on new businesses and ideas, how do you use writing to help crystalize those ideas?

Writing is a main component of my life. Writing sharpens my mind and structures my thinking and this is one expectation my business has from me: to lead with clarity and purpose. We don't lack either.

How important is a business plan these days? The world is changing so fast, do you think it's still an important part of the business journey?

A business plan is a way to articulate your strategic vision as a business. Indeed, the world is changing so fast, but some things remain the same like: building a customer-centric business in order to stay profitable. Serving your clients never goes out of fashion. Simple goals are not always simplistic.

Do you carry a notebook around? How do you write down your ideas today?

I always have something to write my thoughts on. Small notebooks live on my bedside table, in my handbag, in the lounge, in the kitchen and a super-size one on my desk, at work next to my laptop. Because I never underestimate the power of handwriting, even though we run an artificial intelligence business.

FAST TRACK RULE 6

You are not a Manager

ONE OF THE MOST COMMON MISTAKES I see people making in business is the failure to understand the important distinction between a 'leader' and a 'manager'. It's an easy mistake to make, and it's a trap I have fallen into in my own career, but trying to do both is simply not sustainable—in fact, you could be harming the chance of success of your business. Let me explain.

As a business owner and an entrepreneur, you need to remember that you are a leader: it's your idea, your vision and your company. You are not a manager, and quite frankly, you don't really want to be.

So many people get this all confused, and it's a fundamental problem when starting, growing and running a business. Entrepreneurs create change; managers make sure the change happens. It's impossible to do both well.

Management and leadership are both important. In fact, they go hand in hand, but they are two separate functions, carried out by different people. In a business, there should be one leader, many managers and a healthy team. Managers will work 24/7 for you if they believe in and trust you. As I've said before, we don't fly to the moon alone. We need help. Without loyal troops, leaders would be incapable of realising their visions.

As a leader, you need to be good at finding the right people to do the job. Know what the picture is meant to look like and where you want to get to, but don't sweat the detail. That's not your job as a leader.

As a leader of a real estate business, I was good at finding the right people to do the job. I knew what the picture was meant to look like and where I wanted to get to, but I couldn't tell you how to mix concrete, build a wall or even service a hotel. That's not my job, and I hate details. I can do details, but I'm terrible at them. I know that.

After I left Eastern Europe I found myself trying to turn around a country house hotel in England that I had purchased. Funds were low and I couldn't afford to bring in people to help me, so I had to do details. I knew I'd be forcing myself to manage operations, and while I knew I could do it, I also knew I wouldn't do the best job of it.

I spent months doing a lot of things I really disliked before I finally started to bring in the help I needed, and that made all the difference. I recognised that I would eventually need to bring in managers if I wanted to survive. People would tell me "Just teach him to do what you would do" or "show her how to be more organised" but it was easier said than done. Every day, I'd go and do my job, and I was miserable. I was a terrible manager and I knew I was wasting my time. I'd spend half the day thinking up ideas, when I really needed to be working in operations.

Years later, when I invested in a healthy fast food chain in London, I witnessed the same dynamic at work. The owner would try to be helpful by running the register if the store was too busy, dealing with suppliers, working on menus, doing the marketing, working on fit-out with designers and architects and trying to find new locations. It might seem very impressive, but it was simply not a sustainable way to grow the business. Eventually we changed all that, and the business started to achieve the kind of growth it was actually capable of.

If you're going to lead a business, the simple fact is that you cannot mentally and physically do everything well alone, and chances are you don't have all the answers. Attempting to handle everything by yourself will never be sustainable, so for the sake of your business, your personal relationships and your health, don't be afraid to find the people who can give you the help you need.

An entrepreneur is a leader, not a manager. It is just the same as the distinction between an architect and a builder—the architect has the vision and creates the plans, which the builder then follows to make that vision a reality. The architect doesn't dictate to his builder how to mix concrete or lay bricks, but he shares the plan and end vision and then trusts his builder to follow it through to completion.

As a leader, your focus is to create a vision, know the end game and share that vision effectively with your team, investors, bankers and even your customers. But don't attempt to put it into practice yourself. Managers are specialists, and leaders are generalists—we're not wired for details.

Once you're honest about your own strengths and weaknesses, you can recruit people with skillsets you don't have to pick up the details and run with your idea. It's important to find good people to manage operations. Managers make your life easy. You give them the plan; they make it happen. Managers implement systems. They execute and try to improve efficiency in service and production. Managers get the most out of people and processes. Managers make your life easy. You give them the plan; they make it happen.

Once you've found your managers and team, have regular meetings with them to make sure they're doing their jobs. You need to keep sharing the vision with your management team, and you must stay aware of what is happening in the team—both good and bad. Their feedback is vital to enable you to keep making the necessary adjustments on your journey to the end goal.

As a leader, you need to keep your managers motivated to do the nitty gritty work. Once they're in charge of this, you can remain focused on the global view.

FOOTPRINT 6

YOU ARE NOT A MANAGER
TOM BRITTON, CO-FOUNDER SYNDICATEROOM, NON-EXECUTIVE DIRECTOR UK BUSINESS ANGEL ASSOCIATION

Biography

Tom grew up in Los Angeles and completed undergraduate studies majoring in economics, but privately learning as much about the emerging tech world as he could. Once done with University, Tom moved to the UK to test himself as a professional footballer and after a few years in the lower leagues turned his attention to technology as a product manager at TheTrainline. Post deploying the first iteration of their highly successful mobile train ticketing application in 2011, Tom studied for his MBA at Cambridge. That's where he encountered his co-founder of SyndicateRoom and the rest is history being written.

Do you consider yourself a leader or a good manager—or are you both? Can you be both?

As a scaling company, I find that there are situations where I play leader and very few situations where I step in and play manager. I'm a firm believer in self-management and hire people who I know will work hard with very little managerial intervention. My role as leader is very much akin to a product manager's role in a scrum team; to remove obstacles so that the team can work at their optimal level. In that sense, the managing I do is resolving issues, internally or externally so that my team can perform.

As an entrepreneur, you surely must have fallen into the "I can do it all myself" trap? How did you work your way out of that?

When we first started, we very much all believed that we should do everything ourselves. As the team grew, we learned to trust those working with us and shifted responsibility to them. However, when things were not going so well the natural tendency was to shift back to the "I'll just do it" mode—an attitude which is detrimental in many ways as you don't teach the team to resolve the issue and you take time away from the other things you need to do. It's a lose-lose situation.

In today's digital world, do you need leaders or just a bunch of tech-savvy people coming together? How has business changed and how is it always the same?

As we move more into a digital-only world. it's easy to think that tech-savvy individuals are all that is needed in a business. However, a leader will always be needed; someone to identify the most pressing problems and motivate others to solve them. A great piece of engineering means little if there is no-one wanting to use it.

FAST TRACK RULE 7
Living with Uncertainty

YOU NEVER KNOW what's going to happen. That's life. But in business, and in the competitive jungle, not being prepared for change can mean sudden death or worse yet, a long protracted and painful exit. Not knowing can be terrifying.

Of course, we want to avoid both these outcomes at all costs. To do that we need to be awake and we need to be prepared for different scenarios. The trick is not to panic, but to just understand that 'shit happens' and it's not necessarily the shit that matters but how we respond. So, we need a cool head.

At school, we are always taught to be right. Being wrong is a bad thing, and this leaves us with a sense of fear when trying new things, especially in business where mistakes can cost us dearly. As a result, we get stuck and freeze in uncertainty because we don't want to take any chances. Even more so when the landscape is always changing. Today things change so fast that just when we think we have it figured out something new takes place. Back when I was growing our business, I regularly encountered changes in plans. Uncertainly was a daily experience.

Years before, as a young stock broker and trader when the markets crashed in 1982, and the DOW fell 500 points in the biggest single drop in history. I was able to sit back, and not panic. I knew that if I were to sell while everyone else was trying to get through the revolving doors I'd get crushed. I was right. Most of my buddies were all panic-selling and would later get whiplashed when the markets all recovered three days later. Rather than sell, they should have been buyers.

Most people don't like uncertainty, or at least they think they don't like it when in the context of business. But we all routinely deal with it every day in our personal lives. A dog dies, a relative becomes ill or has cancer, you have an accident and the list goes on. While we don't like or expect things like that to happen, we know they are a part of life and we deal with them. We are resilient.

I don't know why, but in business, when something unexpected happens, people often just freak out. There is a bump in the road and suddenly we are all rushing for the revolving doors like the stockbrokers in New York back in '82. It's all a big drama for nothing, and at the end of the day there is always a silver lining for the calm and patient souls. But we have been programmed to react like this, so we need to change the channel.

So, get used to it. Nothing in life is perfect. Sales will rise, and sales will fall. You will do well, and realise you have run out of cash because the growth monkey ate all your money supporting sales. Your top players will leave for better jobs, and they may steal your idea and your customers. You might lose contracts or the markets may change. It's all part of the game. Learn to live with it. Deal with it.

As an entrepreneur, you need to be on guard and watch everything around you and develop an intuitive sense of your business. Eventually it will come. Breathe deep, practice mindfulness, and forget the idea that you can control anything whatsoever other than your own reactions to things. That's just the way it is. And when things are going your way, enjoy them—and I mean really enjoy them, because probably lurking around the corner is another surprise or two.

FOOTPRINT 7

LIVING WITH UNCERTAINTY
JULIA KESSLER, FOUNDER AWARD-WINNING UK DRINKS
COMPANY NIX & KIX.

Biography

Julia Kessler is the co-founder of Nix & Kix. Together with her co-founder Kerstin Robinson, her mission is to remove the stigma and boredom that surrounds soft drinks. For too long, soft drinks have been an ugly sister to alcohol, functional drinks and fresh juices. There's been a lack of imagination, a lack of experimentation and a lack of passion. That's the problem Julia is here to solve.

Before starting the company, she began her career working in operations for large international hardware and software companies and is also a qualified lean startup innovation coach.

How do you handle uncertainty in your business? What are some of the things you do to make sure you aren't totally stressed out?

Uncertainty is part of our day-to-day. Anyone who is running a company relying on moving goods knows that there are a lot of risks involved. Some you can plan for—and some will simply explode. The challenges can vary from a simple damage in transport, to the entire machinery breaking down during the manufacturing process.

A lot of people never go into business because they think they will fail. Being an entrepreneur is about taking risk. How do you minimize risk?

What helps is having a co-founder who compliments you. At Nix & Kix, I look after sales and operations, while Kerstin looks after finance and marketing.

Naturally, I have two conflicting sides. The ops side, which wants to prevent risk and build stock, while my sales side just goes after all opportunities with the tendency to overpromise. Kerstin helps me thinking it through before we end up wasting thousands of pounds.

We minimize risk by looking ahead: market trends, competition, cash flow, inventory management—the whole lot. In addition, we have great friends and mentors who have been very supportive throughout our entire journey.

How does the uncertainty affect your family? Are you able to separate the two and how do you deal with things at home when they go wrong in business?

My top tip for how to deal with uncertainty? I often don't know the answer, so I built a strong network of industry experts. Don't be afraid to ask for their advice, involve your team, get through it and celebrate your success together.

At times when the proverbial does hit the fan, it's difficult to switch off. Luckily, I have a very supportive husband who enjoys brainstorming solutions for the challenges we face. It's not always easy to give the deserved attention to the people you love, so make sure you don't lose them along the way.

FAST TRACK RULE 8

Having Faith

WE ALL NEED TO BELIEVE in something when things get tough. It doesn't have to be religious or spiritual, but having faith in a power greater than yourself is vital if you're going to be a successful entrepreneur.

When I landed in Tallinn on my adventure, I had no idea what my plans were going to be. I didn't know how things would work out. The only thing I knew for certain was that they *would* work out. I didn't know anyone. I had $400 to last me three weeks. But there was something exciting about not knowing anyone in a new environment. I was alone, and yet I knew I was in the right place.

What I learned from this is that if you have faith enough to show up, good stuff happens. Having faith is a key component for your survival. If you try and control everything and everyone, push and force things to work, all that will happen is that you'll be constantly up against the wall, and therefore exhausted. If you can make a leap of faith and trust, however, you no longer have to push; you can pull opportunities and people towards you.

The first step is to find something bigger than yourself to believe in, and trust in something beyond yourself. It doesn't matter whether it's God, a group of colleagues, your family or school, or even your business idea. Leaders are believers: you have to believe in something outside yourself.

The next step is that you also need to believe in yourself, and whatever it is you choose to do. Whatever that is, that is the thing you are meant to do. If you determine you were meant to do something, any obstacle is just an inconvenient annoyance you can get through.

Don't worry about things you cannot control—which is pretty much everything! You have to resign yourself to the fact that you can't control anything or anybody except yourself. The only control you do have is how you respond to things. That's it. Nothing else, so there's no sense in trying. Trust me on this one. So, focus on your own responses.

If you believe in yourself and the vision you have for your life, you'll keep going. Have faith that you are where you're meant to be, and keep going. Faith protects you from the naysayers. Ask yourself: are you confident enough to believe, to take centre stage, to try to do what no one else is doing and ask life for everything? Or are you sitting in the back-balcony section just watching the show? To get started, you need to find the faith to take to the stage with all the lights bearing down on you.

That can be a scary idea, certainly, but in order to succeed, you need to show up and take that first leap forward. If you truly believe in your idea and yourself, you can do it—that's what makes you a leader. In business, as in life, things change, sands shift and suddenly everything can go wrong, but if you believe that your goal is right around the corner, you can stampede through the bandits of your mind. Faith blinds you to "it can't be done". It gives you that craziness that keeps you going. Faith protects you from naysayers and well-meaning friends who don't want you to change.

The great thing is that faith is contagious. Build your business with people who are inspired by your leadership and blind faith in what you are doing. If you don't believe in your idea or yourself—I mean believe enough to bet the ranch and sacrifice precious time that can never be recaptured—don't do it. Leaders are believers, and people follow leaders. Businesses cannot be built without people, so you need to have that blind faith in what you are doing so you can share it. Without that kind of faith, no one is going help you on your journey.

So, decide what you want, and believe you can have it. Even if it seems out of reach at the moment. You have a compass, use it to move in the direction you want to go. It's your intuition.

Life is a decision, and no one can make it but you. Ask yourself if you have enough faith to take a different path and get on with it. You can't read the next chapter if you keep re-reading the last one. Faith gives you the courage to turn the page.

FOOTPRINT 8

HAVING FAITH
MATTHEW BEATTY, CO-FOUNDER & CEO SPACEHOP

Biography

Belfast-born, I'm 30 years-old, living in London. I'm the co-founder of the online marketplace for workspace and meeting rooms, Spacehop.com. I graduated from Queen's University Belfast and worked as medical doctor for five years before deciding to pack it all in and take the path of the entrepreneur.

Do you believe in something greater than yourself and do you think you need faith in business to be successful?

Faith plays a central role in my life as an entrepreneur. Faith is the reason I started on this path and is the reason I continue along it. I am not a particularly religious person and could not turn to religion or some higher being to get me through the tough times; instead, I had to manufacture a belief that everything would work out regardless of the obstacles faced. I did this by focusing on the things I personally could believe in: the business idea, the team and myself. Faith alone will not bring me/us success, but rather it acts as the key motivator and weighs heavily in the decisions I make.

When things are not going in the right direction, what gives you the courage to keep moving forward?

I can say without doubt my journey with Spacehop has been the hardest thing I've ever done in my life. What keeps me moving forward is a combination of things: faith in my business; our passionate team and most importantly the love for what I do. The daily challenges I face as an entrepreneur are extremely motivational for me.

Do you think that faith is just another thing for being stubborn or willful—or is there a difference?

For me, there is a difference. Having faith is the belief in your ability to succeed, whereas to be stubborn or willful are personality traits relating to a refusal to accept failure and a desire to prove others wrong. That's not to say these characteristics don't have a part to play in your success as an entrepreneur. Resilience is a must-have, but it's important for the entrepreneur to realise you're not always right.

PART 2: MONEY

THE WORST THING IN BUSINESS that can happen is running out of cash. This is rule number 1: Don't run out of cash. Whatever happens, without cash you're done. Game over. No cash, no next day.

The startup jungle is merciless. People and companies come and go simply because they don't know how to manage their cash.

We all know most businesses fail and that 90% fail in the first five years! That's an eye-opening statistic if there ever was one. And the sad thing is that most of these businesses fail, not because they don't have good ideas or services, but because they don't know how to manage cash.

Even a growing business can kill you. It might sound strange, but sometimes it's so good it's bad; because as you grow you will need assets and if you don't fund those assets with cash then eventually the growth will kill you.

So, the key is knowing how to manage the cash flow formula, and understanding when and how to raise capital when you need it.

FAST TRACK RULE 9

Managing Money

WHETHER YOU'RE A FRESH-FACED Start Up entrepreneur or an experienced executive, when you start your own business the buck—literally—stops with you. As a leader, you need to know where you are, and only numbers will tell you.

Now, I am not an accountant, but for the last 30 years I've kept an eye on my assets, debt and personal cash flow, and can account for every penny. I look at my personal records every week and do monthly accounts. It keeps me focused and helps me make wise decisions.

I wasn't always like this, however. During my time working as a floor trader on Wall Street, I lived life in the fast lane. My work was stressful and physically demanding, and to deal with that stress, I played hard. I was young and impressionable and was taken in by all the temptations a big city could offer like a kid unsupervised in a candy store. I gobbled up as much as I could, like any child might do. The whole thing nearly killed me. By 1987, I was done. I was burned out, struggling with addictions, unfulfilled and I was broke.

I was then confronted with the harsh reality of the mess I'd made of my life and the amount of money I'd actually wasted. I had received a fat pay cheque every two weeks from the trading company, and that allowed me to be reckless with dinner, cocktails and nightclubs. I was always out having too much fun and not being a responsible adult, so when the debt caught up with me it hit me like a tidal wave.

One day, my then girlfriend (who is now my wife) discovered a shoebox full of bills I had been ignoring—it was case of "out of sight, out of mind". She gave me a great book called *How to Get Out of Debt, Stay Out of Debt, and Live Prosperously* by Jerrold Mundis, and I can honestly say that this was a life-changing moment.

After reading the book, I worked out payment plans with all my creditors, and I stopped being afraid to answer the phone. I also started carrying around a little notebook, and every time I spent money, I'd write it down. At the end of the day, I'd add it all up. Then I started taking those numbers and building a spreadsheet. Over time, that spreadsheet provided me with history, and I could see figures represented as percentages of the total. I could determine if I was spending too much money eating out, on clothes or on groceries, or even if I should be spending more in any of those categories. After a few months, the numbers gave me a true picture of who I was as a person at that time.

Cash flow is simply making sure that the cash going out is less than the cash coming in. It's not accrual accounting, it's cash accounting meaning it's a real-time formula. It's what you actually take in and what you actually pay out. You need to make sure that your out payments are eventually made, and that there is cash to cover bills, but what you want is for cash flow to always be positive.

Cash flow is NOT profit and loss.

You can have a loss in your PL and still have positive cash flow (though you can't do that forever), or you can have a positive PL and run a cash flow deficit. The importance is knowing your numbers; what's coming in and what's going out and managing these numbers so that you are always running a positive cash flow.

I don't carry around a little notebook anymore—although I think my wife would like me to! I do, however, pull all the numbers from my online bank statements. I still take the time to go through the monthly numbers, and I have a cash flow chart that covers more than 20 years of history. I also have a schedule for net asset value, credit cards and debt with rates and payment dates.

Now, I realise that some people may read this and think I am an obsessive. And maybe they would be right, but without these tools, I wouldn't have a clue about where I was, or what I could or couldn't do. And my guess is that if you're not keeping track of your simple numbers at home, you're probably not very good at it in your business. To be a good cash flow manager you need to do this at home and in business.

I believe that if you do your personal accounting for yourself, you're much better prepared to manage the finances of your business. I can't imagine how to do it any other way. As your business grows you will inevitably acquire assets, repay debt, plan holidays and deal with unexpected events, but how can you be expected to make good, informed decisions without all the information? What if things slow down and your businesses goes bust or cannot support you anymore? You can't afford to be blindsided by bad news. I'm a big believer in planning ahead.

As a leader, you need to know where you are, and only numbers will tell you. But I often find that many entrepreneurs rely on cash flow to pay their bills, and that can be a very stressful and dangerous place to be.

So stop. Get a grip on your finances. The first thing is to start with your personal ones. There's no substitute for tracking your own income and expenses. It keeps you focused and helps you make wiser decisions.

As an exercise, try keeping a record of all your expenditure for one month. Put it in a spreadsheet and create a forecast for the next month. Create a net asset value page, which shows your assets minus costs, plus uplifts, minus debt.

Of course, it might not be easy at first, but do it and it won't take long before it becomes second nature, and consequently you'll feel much more in control of your life. And if this habit is ingrained in for your personal finances, then you can apply it to your business finances too.

Once you have a firm grip on the numbers, you can then build an annual cash flow chart—it's a powerful tool for business planning, and it allows you to gain wisdom from seeing the effects of past choices, so you can learn from your mistakes.

An important point to note: take pride in this action. Relish the knowledge you gain by studying the numbers. You're equipping yourself to make wiser choices, and that's one of the biggest, most positive investments that you can make in your business. After all, if you don't understand the numbers behind your business, how are you going to grow it and persuade others to invest their money in it, too?

FOOTPRINT 9

MANAGING MONEY
BRETT ALEGRE-WOOD, ENTREPRENEUR & CHAIRMAN OF GLADFISH, BASTIEN JACK, CASTLEREACH & EZYTRAC

Biography

Brett Alegre-Wood is an Australian-British entrepreneur and author with businesses in Europe, Asia and Australia. He's best-known as a property investor (www.gladfish.com), but his business interests range from tyres, marketing, Amazon, technology and property. He has written more than 20 books as well the winning the People's Book Prize for Non-Fiction. Brett is married with four children under six years of age and lives in Singapore.

Do you do your own financial numbers at home and if so, do you feel that's important?

For the first 10 years of my business, I knew exactly where my cash flow was on a daily basis, I created my own cash flow worksheet that ran all my businesses. Nowadays, my group finance director keeps track of everything, my managing directors keep me updated on progress against KPIs, but I still have full visibility on all the numbers.

How involved are you with managing your businesses finance? Do you review weekly, monthly or how often?

I'm no longer involved daily; I have delegated the responsibility, but I still play an active part in major financial decisions. Being an entrepreneur, I find that I push the finances further than my finance team do, but I like it like that.

Do you believe that the numbers tell all? What do you look for when you analyze your financial statements?

I believe in 'systemizing the routine, humanizing the exception'; I live and die by the numbers. I live in Singapore, away from most of my businesses, so I must rely on numbers to tell me the story. However, numbers never beat picking up the phone or sitting down with the team over beers to get to the bottom of problems. Numbers may identify the problem (or trend), but you still need the human touch to solve most problems.

Do you set targets or budgets each year and how often do you review those?

Absolutely. I am very KPI-driven. I have regular review meetings with management, either weekly, fortnightly or monthly. I have two levels of KPIs: standard, which is normally 5 to 10 specific ones per role and then deeper ones if they fail to meet a standard one; these can run into 50-100 KPIs, but they paint a really good picture of the problem and how to fix it.

FAST TRACK RULE 10
The Winning Cash Flow Formula

RUNNING OUT OF CASH is one of those financial sins we don't want to ever commit. We talked about managing our accounts both at home and in business. But is there a formula that can give us the edge so that our cash flow always stays positive no matter what?

Well, there is a formula that does this. And it's simple to understand. When I first heard it, I had one of those "Ah ha!" moments because it is so simple that it's genius, really.

So here it is: *"Buy Low, Sell High, Pay Late, and Collect Early"* I'll repeat it again just for emphasis; "Buy Low, Sell High, Pay Late, and Collect Early."

Think about it and let it sink in. It's quite brilliant, actually. And while the entire formula makes total sense together, each part is a discussion all in its own. The part that I want to focus on, however, is the last section.

We all are familiar with buying low and selling for more. We all get that. Maybe not to the degree we'd like, but we get it. But the second part is what no one consciously thinks about managing when they're starting out. And if you get this part right, all other things being equal, your cash flow will always be positive.

Managing cash flow is the ultimate financial survival tool. It's about money; how to get it, how to use it, how to collect it and how to spend it. There are thousands of books on accounting if you look for them, and even more on financing. Maybe you've read some of them. But chances are, if you recall, the majority of them are written for salaried financial managers and not for guys and gals who own and manage their own businesses and want to smash it with positive cash flow.

The concept of paying late and collecting early is monumental if you think about it. Huge businesses like grocery store chains with low margins use this formula to a tee. They have long credit terms with suppliers of sometimes 90 to 100 days while collecting for those goods on sale to you in the store on the day. That cash flow float allows them to expand and invest in their business growth.

Here's a simple example; my son has a summer business selling apples. He buys the apples from a local farmer (who only takes cash payment), and then hits up all the neighbours for sales. They know him and they all buy his apples. My son, being the great guy he is, tells his customers they can pay him later at the end of the month which results in his customers always buying more. His sales each month soar. But half way through the month, he's coming to me asking for money to pay the farmer. I ask him why he's broke. He has no idea. His sales are great, but he has no money.

Actually, he needs to reverse the formula. He needs to find another farmer who's going to give him credit and he needs to tell his customers that they either have to pay up front or collect before his payments are due to the farmer.

Having this kind of mindset and financial understanding also helps solve another problem we will address later: how to fund the growth of your business.

It takes money to make money and sales are driven by assets, and the more sales you have the more assets you will need or you will run out of cash. Using the formula allows you to use other people's money (suppliers) while funding the growth of your business. This assumes you have sales and have growth. A business that is failing and uses this formula will only exacerbate the end and create more liabilities on the balance sheet, so use this concept wisely.

FOOTPRINT 10

THE WINNING CASH FLOW FORMULA
NICK JORDAN, CEO TRADE HORIZONS

Biography

Nicholas Jordan is the CEO of Trade Horizons, a company that specializes in helping SMEs around the enter new markets. He has more than 25 years' experience working in US and European Financial Services multinationals, running his own consulting company and startups.

Nick holds a BSc (Hons) in European Business with Technology, a Diploma di Esperto Nella Produzione Industriale and an Executive MBA from London Business School. Nick is also a qualified private banker. He has a strong interest in the London technology startup ecosystem and is a mentor to entrepreneurs, students and charities.

Tell us the difference between cash flow and profit and loss and how people sometimes get that wrong...

Profit and loss is the difference between buying low and selling high. This is your gross margin, the basic component of your profit. The bigger the difference the more leeway you have in incurring other costs to generate and deliver your offering.

Cash flow, at its most basic, is the balance in your company's bank account. If you make a great deal and buy one million widgets for £1 each and can sell them for £5 each you are going to make £4 million pounds in gross margin—a great deal. However, if you need to pay for all your widgets in 30 days and then sell them over the next year you are in trouble. In 30 days, your bank account will be in the red by £1m and only slowly, over the next year, will you recoup your outlay and make your profit. This is a classic cash flow crisis.

How do you manage cash flow in your business?

We do not believe in being late payers. This is not good for your business relationships. The trick therefore is to structure deals with a built-in positive cash flow, a bit like the supermarkets. We look to receive payment from our clients either up front, or in stages, ensuring our costs are covered early and so that any later payments are profit.

What's a great way to improve cash flow and what is a common mistake people make with sales growth and find themselves without cash?

The great dilemma for growing businesses is how to finance growth. This is known as your working capital, the oil that keeps the cogs of your business turning. As you do more business you need more oil. During growth, and even afterwards companies can look at the variety of cash flow finance (invoice financing) options to provide cash against the new business you do.

FAST TRACK RULE 11

Raising Money

UNLIKE THE GARAGE OR RUMMAGE SALE some people do to raise money, we are going to need to go a lot deeper, and very narrow. Our business will need cash. Whether we are starting up and need to build the infrastructure and hire people, or whether we are growing—that cash is being eaten alive and we will need to raise cash. It's part of starting a successful business.

Ask any entrepreneur and they will tell you that raising money can be tough. And the competition for funds from investors is growing every day. Finding an investor isn't impossible, but one thing we need to do as entrepreneurs is find alternative means that will contribute to our financial success.

The first place we should look and any investor will certainly ask, is how much you've invested. You will need to open your own wallet first and tap into savings, home equity, or retirement accounts. Even your kid's candy jar because investors want to see you have "skin in the game". Don't expect others to invest in your startup if you haven't put some of your own money in. Investors favour entrepreneurs with more than "just" sweat equity in the game.

The second thing is to sign up strategic partners early on. There's nothing better than finding a supplier, distributor, or especially a customer who stands to gain so much from your solution that they are willing and able to help foot the bill.

This is a planning-for-success bonus play. When I was building shopping centers in Eastern Europe I was hit with a minor correction in the markets in 1998; the Russian flu, as it was called.

My investor backed off from a commitment to fund the

completion of a big box retail scheme we were developing and I was stuck with a contract to complete and with loans to the bank. My investors were in New York, and no one seemed to care what was happening, nor were they very willing to help. I met with them at a property conference and it was apparent they were willing to write this investment off rather than put more money in. I was devastated. So, I had to think fast and find money under rocks. The most obvious place of course was my main contractor who had as much to lose as I did.

They bailed me out with mezzanine finance, and when the project was completed, I backed in the senior debt from the bank. Everyone got off and even my less than dependable partners benefited.

So just remember that in starting a business you need friends:

— The reliability of your supply sources, whether for materials or software will be key to your success.

— Supplier financing provides invaluable hands-on perspective of what's right in your business and what needs to be changed. These companies will be less focused on final returns and more interested in getting your project finished.

— You can count on early relationships between Start Ups and strategic partners like mine that turn into something really special that endures for years. Like mine did. Once we did the first project like that, I was able to reduce my equity requirements in the future, by going to them and paying a bit more for the cost of funding, but it was short-term and I kept more of the equity.

Finally, you will need to Bootstrap. Paying as you go by earning revenue and managing every dime like it was a dollar is the most cost-effective way to stretch your company's resources—financial and otherwise. Think of the cash flow formula and my son's apple sales. Nothing is more dear than cash when you're starting out. You should never run out of it. The more you can bootstrap in the beginning to achieve good market validation, the easier you are going to find your path to raising capital.

In order to do this successfully you will need to hold fixed costs to a minimum. You need to get good at finding ways to save money and reduce costs. Consider maybe delaying capital purchases, leasing instead of purchasing, renegotiating fees and seeking trade credit terms with key suppliers as examples.

There are no silver bullets when it comes to sourcing early-stage funding, but with the right capital strategy and a concentrated emphasis on bootstrapping, entrepreneurs can avoid shooting themselves in the foot.

FOOTPRINT 11

RAISING MONEY
MATTHEW CUSHEN, CO-FOUNDER WORTH CAPITAL

Biography

A retailer, learning the trade with Woolworths and then the John Lewis Partnership. Now an innovation consultant helping leaders of very large businesses, such as Waitrose, SABMiller and IKEA create new products, services, experiences, brands and strategies.

Having been a serial, and successful, angel investor for 12 years, Matthew co-founded Worth Capital, who run the UK's largest startup funding competition—the Start-Up Series. Winners are given equity funding from a tax efficient fund raised to give investors the opportunity to own a portfolio of the UK's brightest new businesses.

A lot of entrepreneurs will initially raise money from friends and family; is this a good idea and what could be alternatives?

Who'd want to spend precious time with loved ones being quizzed about cash flow or sales growth? Whilst the financial meltdown a decade ago made it even more difficult to get loans from banks, it has created more equity funding alternatives. There are many more angel investors, and brokers to help you find them, an array of different (equity) crowd funding sites and even now-regulated seed investment funds. For those with a product, crowd funding like Kickstarter or Indiegogo can fund your first production run.

As an investor in startups, what first attracts your attention and what do you consider an opportunity?

Market insight. What has the entrepreneur seen in their chosen market to suggest there is an unmet need or desire and what have they done to validate their hypothesis. For example, GÜ puddings saw a gap in indulgent chocolate puddings and they snuck into Waitrose and placed some of their designed packaging (with sand inside for weight) into a fridge, along with a shelf edge price label. They saw customers put the product in their basket (before they apologized and whipped it out again). An unsophisticated experiment—but hugely comforting for investors.

Too many ideas, particularly in the tech space, are great solutions desperately in search of a problem. They might be good ideas, but worthless without understanding why a consumer would care, change behavior and what they would spend.

Once they have your attention, how do successful entrepreneurs close-out getting your funding?

Mostly this is about getting to know the individual or team. Have they evidence of the tenacity, drive and ambition needed to grow a significant business—not just something that will give them an income but create returns for investors? Have they some relevant experience (e.g. in their chosen market or with production)? Are they compelling communicators? They are going to have to sell their product or service to customers and sell their whole business to new recruits and to more investors down the line.

Then there is a bit about the business model and marketing plan—but those are things we can help with. You can't change the entrepreneur or the essence of the market they are looking to operate in.

FAST TRACK RULE 12
Types of Funding

EVERY BUSINESS, no matter the size or industry, has one thing in common: they all have assets, and they need more assets to grow.

All businesses need assets to operate, and there is no getting around this. Whether it is trucks, buildings, people, IT or intellectual property from ideas, the immutable law of successful business operation is you must have enough assets and they must be funded correctly.

Sales at a certain level require a certain level of assets and when sales grow, that asset base must grow with it or a pinch point will come and suddenly, even when things look super great, you will be dead out of money. So, your assets need to grow in proportion to your sales.

So besides needing money, you need different types of money to fund different types of assets.

As we saw in the earlier chapter, an entrepreneur can provide assets by putting in his own money, by raising equity from partners, by using supplier finance and by bootstrapping. All good, but now it's time to get slightly more complex.

There are two basic types of funding for your business: equity and debt. Equity is what you and your partners put in, and debt is what you borrow and pay for. Sometimes.

Traditional debts are interest bearing notes and obligations; normally to senior lenders like banks. But there is also a non-interest bearing debt and that comes from suppliers. This is "free-debt". It's a non-interest bearing liability and as an entrepreneur, this is one of my favourite sources of financing and one which most people do not use enough.

For example, it is common practice for trade to extend

and entrepreneur credit for thirty, sixty and even ninety days to pay their bills. During this time, you have their goods to make sales, and collect. This is free money. And if you look at your own balance sheets you will see a section called "trade accounts payable"—that's where it is! Well-managed businesses can sometimes fund up to 30% of their assets with this kind of credit. Free!

The funding sources are a pretty simple proposition really and there are only three sources for cash to support your business and growth. These main sources are:
— Equity
— Debt
— Free debt

Also, bear in mind on the equity side of the equation there is equity you put in and of course there is retained earnings (equity the business makes when it turns a profit).

If, on the other hand, you are just starting out and are looking for funding then, quantifying its valuation is often an arbitrary, pointless exercise. There may not even be a product in hand, let alone revenue. But you still may need to raise money. This can be tricky and you don't want to give away all your equity before you get out of the starting gate.

Convertible debt (also called convertible notes) is a financing tool that allows Start Ups to raise money while delaying valuation discussions until the company is more mature. Though technically debt convertible notes are meant to convert to equity at a later date, usually a round of funding.

Investors who agree to use convertible notes generally receive warrants or a discount as a reward for putting their money in at the earliest, riskiest stages of the business. In short, this means that their cash converts to equity at a more favourable ratio than investors who come in at the valuation round later.

In the competitive jungle of business, the trick is, of course, not only where you get money and what type of money sources are out there, but also how you manage it.

If you are not managing your equity properly (paying too many dividends out of profit), and not securing and managing free debt to a maximise then you will be putting pressure on your ability to grow your business and feed the beast that wants to eat your cash.

Smart entrepreneurs will know how to do this. They will be aware of a little-known term called "Asset Turns." This needs to become one of the most important financial language terms in your vocabulary because it tells you how many assets you really need at any given point of time. It's a bit like having a compass when you're trying to survive in the jungle. And the equation is simple: it's Sales/Total Assets.

If your business is projected to earn £10,000,000 in sales and you have assets of £4,000,000 then your asset turn is £2.50. That means you are getting £2.50 worth of sales for every £1.00 of assets you have. If your business was growing at more than 10% per year, it would not be able to sustain that kind of growth without more assets. Simple really.

FOOTPRINT 12

TYPES OF FUNDING
DANIEL-IOAN DUMITRESCU, CEO AT RCE & CO-FOUNDER AT ECSIF LTD

Biography

With a PhD. in Cybernetics and Economic Statistics, more than 17 years of experience in the financial field (banks, insurance, guarantee funds, commodities and stock exchanges, money transfer, NPLs, fintech and European funds), Daniel Dumitrescu has worked as Financial Expert of the European Commission and Chief Executive Officer of the Romanian Commodities Exchange in the last few years.

Currently, he is a co-founder alongside Dr. Diana Dumitrescu of the European Centre for Services Investments and Financing, based in London, with the mission of helping innovative SMEs to develop through European and alternative funding by understanding all the requirements and benefits associated with each type of finance.

There are so many sources of funding these days. Can you tell us the top ones you think an entrepreneur should be most familiar with and why?

Crowd funding campaigns allow startups to fund pilot products through online contributions from various retail investors. Being assimilated to a buyer credit, the success or failure of such a campaign offers an immediate feedback on the product, even before spending the money to make the investment. Innovation grants provide young SMEs with the opportunity to support RDI spending for development. A good source of financing for intangible assets, they allow the entrepreneur to maintain control of the company up to a future growth stage.

When you started your business, where did you get your initial funding and how difficult was it?

At first, we used our own savings, self-financing and bank credits. If the access to finance was an easy one due to the macro economic growth trend, the financial crisis has made funding management increasingly difficult. It was then that I realized the importance of understanding the different sources of funding and their characteristics so that they can be evaluated comparatively depending on pros and cons.

Does funding get easier once you have your business in place?

An enterprise at an advanced stage of development has a lower funding risk, being curtailed by various financiers. Compared to a startup, a well-established company benefits from a better negotiating position, enabling it to obtain the most advantageous financing conditions.

Are there different types of funders to approach when your business gets in trouble?

Due to the financial crisis, many SMEs continue to face financial blockages, various public measures have been promoted to address this challenge, such as the EU's recommendation to give entrepreneurs a second chance by encouraging Member States to create public loan guarantee schemes in order to back credits offered by financial institutions to such SMEs.

FAST TRACK RULE 13

Investors

IT'S TOUGH IN THE WORLD OF START UPS and you'll need a lot of help along the way, not least financially. There will come a time when you need an injection of capital into your business to grow it. So, who do you turn to—and, crucially, who don't you turn to?

The answer to the latter question is family and friends. Don't do business with friends you want to keep—falling out over business deals or debt kills friendships. In your quest to raise capital for your new venture, you may be tempted to rely on friends, family and casual acquaintances. Most people think this is the logical place to start. It's not. These are people you sit around the dinner table with, not the boardroom table. What's a more valuable asset in the long run—your business or your friendship? That's a decision you never want to force yourself into having to make.

A good friend of mine and I once bought a business together as equal partners. It all started out fine, but when an opportunity came along to take the business to the next level, I wanted to jump on it and invest more money, and he didn't. As a result, we had a major falling out, our 18 years of friendship were irrevocably damaged and the business quickly suffered too.

So, who do you ask for capital if family and friends are off the table? Answer: you get the money through equity and bank debt.

Equity is the dearest thing, and it's expensive. Don't give it away and don't share it if you don't have to. However, diluting your share of equity is often unavoidable, and you may need to give away some when you need the cash to grow or to get out of trouble.

If you want to go down the equity path, talk to professional investors. They can bring some valuable assets to the table beyond equity, such as experience, wise counsel and connections with other experts. Another important point is that, in my experience, professional or institutional investors are too busy doing deals to want to sit next to you at your desk and question your decisions. Their job isn't to scrutinise the day-to-day details. Even if you need to give a sizeable amount of your shares to private equity investors in the beginning of your business launch, there will be ways to maintain control and claw back your equity as your business improves. As the operating partner, you will always have control over business operations (unless you really screw up), and based on performance, you will be able to earn back more equity as your business grows.

If giving away equity isn't an option, then don't exclude the idea of getting into debt. Go talk to your bank and ask if they have a business-growth lending department. Interest payments can be a drain on cash flow, especially in the beginning if there's too much debt. However, by its very nature, debt is cheaper than equity, so it is usually a better option than selling the majority of your shares. Remember, too: never borrow to spend—borrow to invest.

With both types of investors, be clear about how much money you need now and, if possible, over the next five years. Be sure that you have really gone through the numbers and don't exaggerate. It looks good on paper, but those figures may be an illusion. Equally, there's no point in asking for too small an amount and having to go back, cap in hand, to your original investors—that just looks like bad planning, and reduces any confidence they had in your original plans. Describe at the outset the maximum you think you will need, with an additional percentage for contingency.

Whichever way you decide to raise investment, hire a good corporate lawyer to draft any agreements. A good accountant is also worth their money in gold and can save your headaches with taxes. When you're dealing with professionals, it pays to hire a professional!

FOOTPRINT 13

INVESTORS
DANNY KESSLER, CEO & FOUNDER, THE MET GROUP &
ANGEL INVESTOR

Biography

Danny Kessler is the CEO and a founding member of the Met Group. Since 2002, he has grown it into a diverse organization, involved in a variety of financial services including venture capital, asset management, market making, proprietary trading, regulatory incubation, property development and a host of other innovative business models.

Danny is a passionate entrepreneur and actively helps set up businesses, which he invests in both as principal and passively. He has successfully founded a variety of technology-based ventures. He currently sits on the boards of several rapidly growing companies and has already brokered a number of successful exits in both trade sales and in the public markets.

He is also a widely published underwater photographer who works closely with leading marine research and conservation groups and he has exhibited his images throughout Europe.

When you first started your business how many investors did you have?

We invested our own money to start our own businesses. However, some of the best tech businesses I have been involved with on an executive basis has been where I invested in someone else's business and their vision.

Were they friends and family?

Sometimes they were. I have had mixed fortunes in this regard. I have had some wonderful trusting and heart-warming experiences where only the comradery and knowledge of where you're from and where you are going to has enabled the success we have achieved. In one case this was all the way from seeding a business to selling it to a NASDAQ listed company for $232m. Conversely, I have experienced old friends who have become bitter and jealous, unable to contribute as much as one would have hoped leading to a breakdown of the relationship and irreconcilable position.

How did you communicate with your investors and how often?

I believe monthly communications on tactical matters where there have been changes, otherwise this is not necessary as investors should trust those they are backing and quarterly communications on strategic issues.

One of the biggest problems is a misunderstanding between entrepreneurs and investors. How can that be avoided?

Clearly, the best investors invest in the talent of the team and in particular, the founder/leader. They understand that the best people are the most vital ingredient in determining the success of their investment. If the talent they wish to invest in is placed in a large scalable market opportunity, then they should trust them to find the best product/service fit. Normally, as a rule of thumb in my mind, 60% of their investment is in the team, 25% in the market opportunity and 15% in the product/service fit. So, ultimately, they must buy into the talent they have invested in and understand their vision which has to be clearly understood and communicated between founder and investor. A good investor will support the vision of the founder and allow them the flexibility to pivot as no-one can see across the chessboard from the outset. At the same time, a good leader of the business must be willing to listen to the investor's views and incorporate these when they have value. So. in a nutshell, investors need to trust those they are backing and their vision, be flexible and patient, but honest and candid, whilst giving the talent time to breathe and focus on what matters in an environment of clear communication. Anything else is likely to lead to failure. It's not too dissimilar to being a parent!

FAST TRACK RULE 14

Money Under Rocks

MAXIMISING RETURNS is about using leverage. Bank debt. Money that is cheaper than the margins you make on your product or service. You need cash to grow your business whether you are making doughnuts, or bicycles or building a shopping centre in Kenya or London. As you've no doubt heard, "it takes money to make money".

All businesses need assets to operate and assets cost money. The foundation of any company is its assets. People or trucks, they are assets and you need them. So, it's sensible to assume that if your business is growing you need more of those things called assets. If that weren't the case, Apple could have stayed in Jobs' garage, and he and Steve Wozniak could have delivered their computers in the back seat of their VW Beetle.

There are only two ways really to fund that growth: 1) your money, or 2) other people's money. Equity is your money. Money you put in the business, normally at the beginning.

There is only so much you can put in, so let's examine the other part of the funding structure: Other People's money.

Back in 1998 when the Asian flu or Russian Currency crises hit Europe, the wheels almost fell off the bus. Banks stopped lending, investors ran for the hills. I was in the middle of a project building a DIY warehouse for a large German retailer. I was half way in the deal, with a completion date around the corner in six months. But my equity partner refused to fund and like many institutional investors reacted and simply wanted to sell the asset. Sell to whom?

I had a problem. No one in my community knew my investors in New York, but they knew me and a failure of this magnitude would not be well received by anyone, especially my banks. Therefore, I had to find the solution.

I approached the guys with almost as much skin in the game as me; my contractors. You see over the years, I had built up a good relationship with them and we had done many projects together and they knew there would be many more. They provided me the mezzanine finance and construction loans to get through to completion where I could then go to my bank for senior take out debt.

This is just an example, but when the environment turns upside down, or even when small things appear that are unexpected, sometimes you need to find short-term bridge financing that can take you to the next step.

Today I see banks turning off the light switches and curbing lending other than senior take out. They are risk averse again, and don't want to be part of the value add equation in lending. This is now being taken up by Private Equity and Specialist Debt houses. Find out who they are and what sectors they focus on because these funders will be your new best friends in many cases. Equally, the advent of crowd funding and Peer2Peer lending have taken up the slack.

I recall when we were growing our restaurant chain in London that we needed cash fast to grow our acquisitions of new sites. The banks were not keen to take that value add risk and there were few alternatives. Crowd funding was one of them. But this was in the early days, and my partner thought it gave our business a stigma of desperation. He was wrong. It was a quick and easy source of capital and we could have moved rather quickly. Instead we finally decided to pursue our longer-term bank solution which in my opinion put us 18 months behind.

So, it's there—you just need to find the rocks and look under them.

FOOTPRINT 14

FINDING MONEY UNDER ROCKS
MARTYN HODGSON, CEO OF SWIRRAL & NON-EXEC FD VARIOUS TECH FIRMS

Biography

Martyn has a keen interest in the impact of technology and automation on the future. He works with ambitious technology companies, particularly ones who are looking to disrupt their industry. He acts as virtual finance director for several companies, supporting their funding, growth plans and strategy and has co-founded a healthtech and a fintech company. He's a qualified accountant having started life with a small Scottish practice, then moving to Ernst & Young before moving to industry in commercial finance director roles.

When you were starting out in business, did you ever have a moment when the plan went wrong and you were suddenly left short of cash? Tell us about that...

In one of my past businesses, we got too engrossed in developing the product before thinking it was ready to launch. We hung too much reliance on getting outside funding which didn't happen. It's easy now to look back in hindsight, but we should've been looking to form business partnerships and develop more channels to sell what we had at the time—which was pretty decent. Present a duck on water and they look to be gliding along effortlessly, but under the water the feet are kicking madly!

How did you solve the problem?

For this business in question we ran out of cash for development and the work that should've been done to develop the partnerships was started too late. Several members of the team decided they had to bring in some regular income, which led to the break-up of the core team.

What kind of creative off-piste financing have you ever done that may have bridged a problem?

I'll illustrate this with one client who had over-expanded and was indebted and trying to trade his way out of trouble. To obtain additional cash, there was a lot of belt-tightening that could be done without compromising the business trading before seeking funding from outside. Beyond that, those suppliers or customers who were strategically aligned to my client were approached to provide some financial assistance, given the mutual benefit of doing so.

PART 3: SCALING

BUILDING A BUSINESS requires people. You can't do this alone and if you try it will never grow and you will be constantly frustrated. You need to scale in order to make your business work. No one travels to the moon alone. We need the ground crew behind us.

The problem is most people don't know how and they think they can't afford it. They do everything themselves thinking they will wait until more money comes in. Then they will scale. Of course, that never happens, because oddly money has a mind of its own, and even as sales will rise a bit it will have found other uses.

So you need to just grit your teeth and take the leap of faith and do what you know deep down you must do.

Whether it's buying equipment or hiring people it's the same. You can't afford not to hire the right people. Think of it this way: you don't pay salaries all in one go. You pay them month by month. And if you don't see results, you can let the person go.

FAST TRACK RULE 15
How to Build a Winning Team

WHEN I ARRIVED in Estonia in 1992, I only had $400 to my name. I didn't know anybody in Tallinn, I knew nothing about the local market, and to be honest, I knew very little about real estate. Over the course of the next 16 years, however, I went on to build real estate businesses worth $200million that would employ more than 850 people in 35 different offices across Eastern and Central Europe.

The key to my success was finding the right team. I recognised that not knowing the industry, the language or the market was going to be challenge, but I was an entrepreneur with a vision, so I found the right people to make that vision a reality.

Whatever your industry, finding and building the right team will inevitably become a crucial part of your own business success. Remember, even the greatest astronauts don't fly to the moon alone. In order to reach their goal, they have a team of skilled specialists behind them, and in just the same way, every successful entrepreneur needs a great ground team, too.

It is important to recognise the need for a team early in the life of your business. Trying to do everything yourself simply isn't sustainable, and if you are too far down the line before you realise this, you may find it very difficult to restructure. Gathering the right people around you can help you to achieve your business goals quicker, and with a more solid foundation for long-term success.

The first thing to do is take a step back from your business and ask yourself what are its most important components. It's your baby so you probably know it inside out, but try to look at the company with fresh eyes as if you know nothing. Steve Wozniak knew about computers, Steve Jobs didn't. They recognised this from the start, and the Apple success story was only possible by combining their separate skillsets.

Now, identify jobs roles that need to be filled. You will need key employees to manage each of the critical functions of your business, with people you can rely on to carry out your vision and execute the day-to-day work. It is important to learn to delegate and trust in others, so rather than trying to stay involved in every aspect of the business, just meet with your managers regularly to stay updated.

Besides your internal team, you will need to build a team outside the company. Most people call this networking, but if you do it right you can see these people as an extension of your business that may, at times, be even more important than your internal team.

As I grew my business, I worked with lawyers, architects, publicists, accountants and construction companies, all of whom were external but added invaluable specialist skills to my organisation. It's worth hiring the best, and even keeping them on a retainer, as long as you believe they will really add value.

Your team should have skills you don't have, but it's also important that you like them as people. Execution is key for Start Up success, and personality clashes can be a harmful and costly distraction. You can quickly spot whether someone is going to blend in with others or if they're difficult. If they don't fit in, let them go, and find new people. It might sound brutal, but you can't be trapped by personalities and loyalty. Give a new employee a fair and thorough try, of course, and start by being specific about what they need to do. If they struggle to do their job well because they simply don't know what they're doing wrong, bring in someone to help them. If that fails, there is only the door. You'd be surprised how many entrepreneurs get tied to ineffective staff because they like them or feel bad about firing someone. You're in business to create, build, and add value. Don't waste your time. Only keep staff members who are determined to work hard and care about success.

Keep doing this until you put together the right team. You will spend a lot of your time with these people—in fact, probably more time than you spend with your own family—so it is important you enjoy each other's company or it will not be sustainable.

So, finding the right team is crucial to your success. And as it's a long, hard process to find the right people, once you have them, it's also important to retain them and maintain good relationships. You can do this in a number of ways.

Firstly, pay them well. When you're hiring, it can be tempting to drive a hard bargain and get new team members to agree to lower levels of pay than they might be hoping for in order to save a few dollars each month. Of course, you need ensure whatever you pay your staff is commercially viable, but remember that you want motivated staff that are excited about the opportunity and a fair level of pay goes a long way to achieving that.

Then train them and give them the tools for success. Good employees and managers are determined to succeed, both for your business and on a personal level. Do everything you can to encourage that determination by creating a clear opportunity for progression. You don't want valued team members to have to look elsewhere for their next career challenge, so a clear vertical ladder of progression can be a great motivator.

If your team is excited and willing to work hard, they never watch the clock. Ultimately, everyone is looking out for their own interests in life, so you want joining your team to be an exciting opportunity for them personally. They need to be proud of their jobs, and to care about what the customers think. If the staff don't want to work, if no one cares about service or quality, or if people are only interested in their pay cheque, the success of the overall enterprise flounders.

It's also crucial to reward your team. Celebrate successes and build camaraderie through work and play. Personal touches such as holding birthday parties in your offices, putting on weekends away or just having fun will build loyalty.

Put on annual awards evenings and give out trophies for the best salesperson and best employee, with prizes for some goofy things as well. These little things add up to make a big difference by creating a human, emotional connection. Over time, your staff will become one big family who are ready to work together towards your shared goals. Not only does this make business sense, keeping staff turnover to a minimum and increasing efficiency, but you also never know when your team will really bail you out.

FOOTPRINT 15

HOW TO BUILD A WINNING TEAM
TIM BETHEL, CEO & CO-FOUNDER AT JDX CONSULTING, DIRECTOR AT THE COLUMBO GROUP

Biography

Tim began working in the City of London in 2002 when he worked for an asset management firm. In 2004, Tim joined a startup; The Derivatives Consulting Group—DCG—run by Jonathan Davies (JD), as the first employee and went on to become Global Head of Benchmarking and Client Executive for a number of major US investment banks. In 2007, Tim moved to New York to open the North America office and stayed through the acquisition by Sapient in 2008. In 2012—and back again in London—Tim set up JDX, back with JD from DCG, and is now the CEO.

When building your business, how many were you when you started out and how fast did you grow over what period of time?

It was just myself and JD on day one! Today, just five years later, we have more than 450 employees across three continents.

What was the most important thing when building your team? Did you have events, parties, awards? Was it like a family or did people just clock in and out?

We knew we had to develop a strong culture from day one, so we hired people with big personalities and tremendous ambitions. The culture we wanted was one where our employees felt valued, trusted and had fun—it's cliche, but it works—only when it's done right and for that to happen it has to be genuine. We have an extensive training programme, we promote aggressively from within, we socialise outside of work hours—karaoke, sports teams, trips, black tie dinners and so on. We reward high performers and we include all our staff in developing our strategy. In all of these things, both JD and I are always involved.

How did you get people on board to work 24/7? You must have had a vision or a purpose. How was that communicated?

Our vision was important, but I've never been one to be too wed to any one idea—you need to adapt and to never stop challenging your business strategy. The key to get people all on board, though, is communication. Over-communicate if you have to. Bring your staff into the fold as early as possible as things develop. That's not to say that business is a democracy, but if you don't get your employees bought into your vision and your business plans, then how are you realistically going to execute on them?

How is the best way to keep key people and do you share your success with them as part of that?

Make them feel valued. Trust them. Reward them. And make sure they share in the success of the company—be that shares or share options. One of the main reasons people leave a firm isn't their role or the company—it is because of their manager—so we make sure we manage our people effectively, and most importantly, we train our staff extensively in how to manage people themselves so we can retain talent at every level of the organisation.

FAST TRACK RULE 16

Why You Need to Hire

MOST ENTREPRENEURS are matter of fact, anyone starting in business is faced with an immediate cash flow issue. Spending money on growing or saving, building up cash reserves and saving 10%, and then spending; kind of like grandmother would have advised years ago..

Problem was, smart as my grandmother was, she was not an entrepreneur or building a business. But the intuitive idea that prudence in spending is good is inherent in all of us and as a general rule is a good one to follow. That said, there are times when it can be misleading or simply plain wrong.

When you are building a business, no matter what it is, you won't know everything there is to know, and you won't have the time to do everything either (more on this in the next chapter). The 10,000-hour rule that we have all heard about which we need to make us experts doesn't apply in business in my opinion, but if you don't need to know everything, then you need others around you who do. If not, you will be frustrated that things are not getting done when you know that they should.

Most entrepreneurs starting out will think they can't afford to hire. They will wait until some sales start to come through the door; they will trudge on by themselves. The fact is, they cannot afford not to hire, because time is money and waiting around for something like sales to happen is like burning time and money. And you will never be able to capture that time back again. Furthermore, as all ideas are universal, if you're not at the forefront then someone else will be.

Think of it this way; you don't need to pay salaries up front all at once. You pay people monthly and normally will have a three-month probationary review so that if it doesn't work out you can fire them. So, if someone's getting paid $35,000 per year, while actually that may sound like a big number for a Start Up business, in fact it's less than $3000 per month. If the results from having this person around don't develop after three months, then they are gone and you will have spent $9000 and probably gotten at least something out of the whole exercise.

The point is, you need to see results. And the other point is the larger and scarier the number is, the faster those results should come. I would expect someone earning $100,000 per year to be able to come and make almost an immediate difference to the operation compared with someone at $35,000.

Therefore, hiring to grow is crucial and a necessity and cannot be skimped on. Skimming will only keep you small, and worse, skimping will not allow you to learn and fill the knowledge gaps in the business. That's worse than saving the money because it's the knowledge base—or lack of it—that will make or break fast forward movement of your business and help you stand out.

Again, I'm not saying grandmother was wrong in her prudent investment advice, I'm just saying that to be successful you cannot know everything and of course you cannot do everything yourself, which is the next skill we need to talk about now...

FOOTPRINT 16

WHY YOU NEED TO HIRE
JÜRGEN M KOPELKE, CEO & CO-FOUNDER
WEBUMBRELLA

Biography

Based in Berlin, entrepreneur, business leader and international sales executive who enjoys building high growth and innovative businesses which contribute to real disruptive change, Jürgen M Kopelke is CEO and co-founder of Webumbrella. He is continually learning and amazed about the possibilities of unleashing the power of talented and passionate people. Jürgen has founded four companies, is an expert in SaaS and e-commerce and a mentor at Startup boot camp and InsurTech. He is also an ambassador for Global Startup Awards CE.

When you were growing your business, when did you decide you needed more people around you to help?

Because Webumbrella is a rather complex SaaS solution for e-commerce companies—thus a b2b business—it was absolutely clear to hire people once the solution was ready for market. Beside of this, I freed 50% of my time by outsourcing all accounting, payroll and tax stuff to an external provider from the very beginning. Especially because of focusing on my own strengths and regarding efficiency, that was a logical decision.

Who were the first key people you hired and why? Were you skeptical about the costs?

First we hired one person for the development team and one UX designer in order to finalize product development. And then—some three months later—we hired two people for marketing, sales and sales support. The resulting personnel costs had already been considered very carefully in the planning phase.

If you had to do it all over again, would you hire faster and more people?

I think we did pretty well because you have to be very clear from the first moment onwards in your business development regarding whether you want to or you have to hire people. Finding and getting the right people on board is always a process of some weeks—up to months sometimes—and this process needs to be prepared and executed thoughtfully.

Why do you think entrepreneurs try and do it all themselves and were you the same at the start?

Sometimes entrepreneurs are not very experienced with delegating and in some cases, they are afraid about the additional cost and the respective admin work related to having employees that need to be managed, somehow. What I've learned is that you must be very careful about who you get on board. At the beginning of a company's development, mistakes in hiring can be fatal because they are rarely quick to repair and can cost valuable time.

FAST TRACK RULE 17
Delegation

THIS IS PROBABLY one of the most important chapters. It works alongside hiring, but stands above almost everything else you can ever talk about regarding a business. Once you have your "why" and have that all written up and are communicating the purpose and mission to customers and employees, then this is really what you now need to focus on immediately.

I found this skillset secret totally by accident, which is probably why it's such a gem and no-brainer, really. It's one of those things that if you just think about it makes all the sense in the world and when executed simply can have an immediate and explosive impact.

So, let me tell you how that happened in the first place…

If you've read my other book, "Why Sell Tacos in Africa", you will know I found myself in Central and Eastern Europe starting a new business, almost by accident as well. I was in countries I knew nothing about, and I could not speak the local languages; Estonian, Latvian, Lithuanian, and Polish. How was I ever going to build a business, let alone build a business in all these separate and very different cultures and with different languages? It was a challenge.

I was building apartments at the time for embassy personnel and I would have to meet with the local builders. It was a nightmare trying to get them to understand anything. I even had one situation where I had a US embassy personnel moving in to a flat in a week, and when I went to the final site meeting I realised that the contractor had failed to put in lights! Can you imagine? Simply because we could not communicate with each other.

From that day on, I hired local people who spoke English (mostly I could not afford) and that was the beginning of everything. In fact, what I did was what I was supposed to do; get business and guide the ship. I did the planning and hired people for everything simply because I could not communicate in the local language.

The funny thing was that had I been in New York, or Chicago where I could speak the language, I would have tried to do everything myself like any good entrepreneur starting out. But here in Eastern Europe, I had no choice. I had to hire or I had to close shop. It was either or and that made all the difference.

Even my local competitors fell into the "I can't afford to hire" trap and I just blew by them in a very short time, because hiring people to do the operational functional aspects of my business allowed me to explode and grow faster than anyone else.

I told you it was simple.

But it's not easy to do.

You will think you cannot afford it; you will think you need to know everything; and you will think intuitively that you must do everything yourself. That's how we all think in the beginning. And that makes us like everyone else, and then we drift along until we sink and become part of that business failure statistic we hear about so often.

Think of a band. Four members; guitar, bass, drums, singer and maybe a second guitar or a piano. There isn't just one guy up there. There are four or five, and each are contributing something special, something none of the other can do. And the result could be some amazing music.

So get some faith, find the "why", create a mission and purpose then go out and hire experts and delegate everything you can with you at the forefront, banging the drum and leading the way. If you do that, you can even have a mediocre business or idea and it will be a smashing success.

FOOTPRINT 17

DELEGATION
ADAM GORDON, CEO & CO-FOUNDER CANDIDATE.ID

Biography

Having worked at international marketing group Havas and in consulting at PwC, Adam Gordon noticed employers weren't taking advantage of social media for talent acquisition, so created Social Media Search in 2009. After three years serving international employers, Adam took the company into a joint venture with Norman Broadbent plc. In 2016, he undertook a management buy-out and merged SMS with recruitment tech startup Candidate.ID which he had co-founded in his spare time. Candidate.ID was listed as one of the 10 most disruptive technologies in HR in 2016, one month after launching, and works with employers including Accenture, Mondelez, QuintilesIMS, Thermo Fisher Scientific and WPP.

As a business owner, do you find it hard to delegate?

As a business owner you will limit your company's growth potential if you can't delegate. That's obvious, but we normally still find it hard to pass on tasks. The old saying 'if you want a job done right, do it yourself' might seem true, but it's very counterproductive when trying to build a company. I have certainly found delegating hard and have been called a control freak on many occasions, but it's less frequent every year as I learn to let go.

How do you let go and let people crack on knowing they're going to make mistakes? Do you jump in and help them, or employ other methods?

As your business grows, you need to keep shedding tasks and either up-skilling your team or hiring in skills so you don't become a bottleneck. I tend to throw people in at the deep end and see how good their swimming is. I do warn them in advance, though; otherwise they could be shocked or demotivated.

How do you keep track when you delegate?

You need to ensure you have robust project management systems and technology in place to help you run your business effectively. As your company grows, you need to appoint managers so you aren't managing everyone. That filter creates control.

When you first started out, how many people do you have in your business, and did you delegate things early on or were you doing everything yourself? When did that change?

When I first started my business in 2009. there was only me so I had to do everything—but quickly, I needed to hire and I specifically looked for someone with all the skills I don't have. Like many business owners, I'm a salesman and not a great project manager, so my first hire was the opposite of me.

What have you learned about growing a business and people by allowing yourself to delegate more?

You can scale much faster when you let go of operational activities and focus on the things that only you can do, which may be surprisingly little. Don't live inside your business. Sit on top of it.

FAST TRACK RULE 18
Fast is Better Than Slow

IN 1992, I MET A MAN known only as 'Elvis' in an Estonian sauna. In no uncertain terms, Elvis warned me never to commit to a deal if Finnish businessmen showed interest, because they always enter the market too late. They want total governance, total transparency and everything needs to be de-risked. Naturally, I forgot his fleeting comment almost immediately.

Fourteen years later, my property development firm was booming. It was 2006 and in the small countries of Central and Eastern Europe there was a tidal wave of cash pushing yields to record lows. With values soaring, I was running around London lining up queues of investors for a property fund. I also had a target of purchasing a publicly traded company in Helsinki, but one day, out of the blue, I got a call from a Finnish private equity firm asking about a business of mine they wanted to purchase. The words of Elvis suddenly came flashing back, and alarm bells rang in my head.

With little more than a hunch, and despite an explosive market, I made the sudden decision to fold. At the time, it seemed liked madness but for the next year and a half, I sold off my businesses one by one. Just as the last company sold in 2008, the crisis hit, and the economy crashed. The music had stopped, but I was out watching the values plummet all over the world.

Whether you call it instinct or just luck, I was suddenly a guru. The fact is, if I had sat back and procrastinated, waiting for everything to be absolutely perfect, my story would have panned out very differently.

Unfortunately, the tendency to procrastinate is something that I see all too often in business. When I was a futures trader on

Wall Street, I learned that you need to take decisions quickly—if you're wrong you can always correct your course. If you don't, you're stuffed; hanging on to a losing position hoping it will turn around. So, move quickly and make decisions; lots of them.

I think in some ways procrastination is ingrained into us from school age. Teachers grade our work based on if we have the right answer, so our mindsets are naturally focused on knowing all the answers before committing. Consequently, we fear failure and ridicule for getting it wrong, and the desire to protect our sensitive egos becomes a great excuse to never even get started.

Successful entrepreneurs are those who have committed to plans and made decisions. They don't waste too much time listening to other people's opinions, weighing up and considering pros and cons. They don't dither, waver and vacillate. They trust their intuition. And once committed to a path, all kinds of doors have opened up for them.

My guess is that you may probably have an idea for your business that you're hesitant about. You're probably concerned it won't work, you're not ready or you need more information. This is how most of us operate—we hate the unknown so we let things carry on as they are.

The thing is, however, since most people think that way, anyone who thinks differently and just tries begins with a distinct advantage. They are far down the road before anyone else gives it a go.

Every journey starts with a step. That's it. Only one step. Just like your first tentative dive off a diving board, your business venture doesn't need to achieve gold medal perfection at the start—that will come with time.

To avoid procrastination and move quickly, you need to decide what you want to achieve. Remember, your circumstances are unique, so look at the opportunities available to you. Create a vision for your future and commit to it.

In the beginning, it's easy to make mistakes because they don't cost much. In those early stages, it's easy to shut down the whole thing and walk away if it doesn't work. But the key is to start. Just start, and don't worry if you don't have all the answers.

Learning as you build is an invaluable process. If you find you're wrong, you can adjust until you get the model right. Starting small means you are flexible, and there's little to lose. You can always start over again. Just don't overthink things. Every time you hit a roadblock, you try another way. But you keep on going.

FOOTPRINT 18

FAST IS BETTER THAN SLOW
ROBERT ATKIN, FOUNDER & CIO APEXX FINTECH LTD

Biography

Qualified as air traffic engineer and then became a concert promoter as his first business venture, promoting an Elvis Costello gig. Robert signed bands for Warner Bros; set up RAM Records, a music publishing company and has worked in the US and Sweden. He has sold cars, set up a phone company, become a leading Vodafone distributor. He also set up Knowledge Management, The Music Engine and held a host of other high profile roles as well as being ecommerce manager at The Imperial War Museum before moving into fintech development.

In today's fast-paced world of business, how do you create and build a business quickly?

Make your own decisions quickly (who knows more about your own skills and knowledge than you?). Find creative people in development, in art, in design: delegate, delegate, delegate and coordinate. Have fun doing it and don't employ dull people. Learn to read people and learn to listen; see what isn't written.

Have things moved on too fast; do you think entrepreneurs should slow down and stop chasing too many balls, or is that a good thing?

Entrepreneurs have no choice other than to run fast; the rest of the world is, and if you don't, you'll be left behind and it's getting faster all the time. Make things that can assist, speed and reduce costs.

How many new ideas do you have going at any one time and is that difficult to manage?

Dozens—approximately one dozen active at any time and it's not difficult to manage if you have the resources and can delegate to a great team. Research and pick the winners to focus on! Network widely. Then sell hard, use channel partners to broaden your reach.

How important is building quick teams to tackle and prove concepts?

It is essential to build teams that magnify your capacity.

FAST TRACK RULE 19

Build a Brand

AS A LEADER, YOUR NEXT STEP is to turn your vision into a business and that business into a brand. Numbers, profits and cash flow are all important, but the fact is that people will often be drawn to you initially, and keep coming back, because of your brand.

Think of some companies that are household names across the globe, such as Apple, Facebook or Google. I bet that straight away you picture the brand and the logo before you see anything else. Correct? You could probably even identify some of the world's best brands based only on the font they use.

In today's digital age, attention spans are getting shorter so you are lucky to hold someone's attention for two minutes. Therefore, for your business to succeed, you need to really grab people and get above the noise in your sector. You need to stand out — just like those household names. You need people to identify with the core values of brand, to see it in their mind's eye, to recognise it in less than a second. If you can do that, you've added tremendous value to your business and set yourself up to grow rapidly. And, importantly, you need to be able to do that in whatever country or sector you're in.

So how do you rise above the noise? Think about a name, a look, a colour, but make sure it reflects and represents who you are and what you're trying to achieve. A good example is when I came up with a brand for my real estate company in Central and Eastern Europe. I combined mine and my wife's surnames, Oberschneider and Hauser, to create Ober-Haus. The beauty of this name was that it worked well as a German name (meaning House of Lords) across multiple countries that, while they all spoke different language, all had Germanic linguistic roots. My competitors all had local, bizarre-sounding names that, while good in one country, could not transfer to other countries. Ober-Haus, on the other hand, would translate well in every country. It was perfect for a cross-border real estate company, it had the right level of prestige and it suited our vision. That was our advantage.

If you're lucky, you might stumble on your brand one night while watching TV, which is what happened to me with Ober-Haus. Alternatively, there are many good brand consultancy firms who will help to squeeze it out of you. Either way, it needs careful consideration and a little creativity because will need something unique and attention grabbing to make yourself visible.

You then need to clarify your offer and think about what you do. Be clear about your product or service. A simple message works best—can you sum up your product or service in three or four short words? Most of the world's best brands can.

It's vital to also use your brand to emphasise your USP. Look at the competition, and consider how crowded the market is. Identify the aspect of your business that uniquely identifies you, that distinguishes you from the rest of the market. Generally, the key to building a strong brand is to provide some kind of pleasurable experience or solve a distressing problem for your customers. Your brand needs to convey that people will get either pleasure or a solution from you.

Once you have figured out your brand, build on it. Build that brand into everything you do, from email signatures to internal communications to marketing campaigns. Broadcast it on a consistent basis until you build recognition in the market. Whether you're doing it digitally, making calls or putting up posters, building any brand takes time, and you need to be consistent with your messaging.

You may want to consider hiring an agency that can help you get the word out in a targeted way. You don't need to know how to do that—remember, you're the entrepreneur with the vision. Your job is to make sure others communicate your vision in the best way possible.

A brand can — and should — lead the business; it can even loom larger than the business itself. If you can do that, you've added tremendous value to your business and set yourself up to grow rapidly. And when it's time to exit the market, it's that brand, as much as anything else, that buyers will be purchasing.

FOOTPRINT 19

BUILD A BRAND
RICHARD CORBETT, FOUNDER & CEO EYETEASE

Biography

Richard Corbett is the founder and CEO of Eyetease. Famed for creating the world's first digital rooftop advertising technology for taxis and first in-vehicle high speed Wi-Fi technology from the age of 24 years old, Corbett is an entrepreneur who promotes passion, creativity and disruptive thinking.

Initially a bootstrapped entrepreneur with no external funding, Corbett's innovations have helped him grow Eyetease organically into a global multimillion-dollar business. Today, Corbett is ranked in the top 100 UK entrepreneurs by The Times and top 60 tech influencers by The Evening Standard. Notably, Corbett's company "Eyetease" has been featured on Virgin.com and endorsed by Richard Branson as an example of "how to create the perfect brand name for your startup".

What does branding mean to you and how important is it?

A great business is 50% "perception" and 50% "quality". You can have the best product in the market, but unless the market perceives this to be the case, you're only halfway to having a great business. Perception is built wholly through your branding! So how important is branding? Perilously important!

If you had to start again, where would you put branding as a priority?

The brand for me has always been the gel that holds the business together and helps execute your strategy. Once you have your product sorted, you've identified your target customer, you've assessed the competition and you've nailed your business model—the brand should wrap this all together in a beautiful bow.

When you are branding, are you doing this yourself, or do you find professionals to help and how do you find them?

When starting a new business, or creating a brand from scratch, I like to be involved in the process. I have three strict rules that I must follow:

1. Be able to buy the dot com—which pushes my creativity to the max!

2. You must have a name which follows two syllables. Ever wondered why many of the world's biggest brands are two syllables?—Face-book, App-le, Goo-gle, e-bay…? Just a thought!

3. Branding my B2B business like a B2C company. Why? Everyone's a consumer, even if they sit in a big office.

I've heard it said that the brand should be bigger than the business; do you agree with that and why?

Yes, but to a point! Be careful that you do not become an empty vessel—by this I mean, you make a lot of noise. but you have no substance. Entrepreneurs will always make the brand bigger than they are with the hope of growing into the brand. A wise friend once told me to "fake it till you make it"—she is now my wife. Ensure you do not misrepresent the business by over-promising and under delivering—this is neither an ethical or sustainable business strategy. Remember this, a great brand will get one sale, but a great business gets the repeat orders and growth! Ensure you have the quality to match the perception!

FAST TRACK RULE 20

Build Baskets

AS AN ENTREPRENEUR, you're always looking ahead at the possibilities. You connect dots and lines where others don't see them. Your ability to do this means that there will be lots of opportunities to diversify your first business and create different 'baskets'.

If your core business idea is a good one, it may well have more potential angles and applications than you first imagined. You may quickly find opportunities to expand what you are already doing into another related business, which gives you diversity, spread risk and a second source of income.

Of course, your first business is likely to be your most important asset. This is the baby that will make or break you, so your focus should be on building a team and a brand, rolling out your product or service and working to get the execution spot on. At some point, however, you'll see that there are other aspects of your business that can be divided, or at least segregated, into separate businesses.

An example of building baskets is when I was building, renovating, and renting apartments, and it became apparent that I needed someone to manage them. In a light bulb moment, I realised that other developers and property owners might like to use a management service too. So I built a property management services business.

As my agency business grew, and we sold homes to people, I found that we often had clients that didn't fit the lending criteria of the local banks. Naturally, we wanted to increase sales, so I started a mortgage company to help our clients buy homes.

By 2008, I had a retail and commercial real estate agency business, a residential and commercial property management services company, a mortgage bank, a development company and a chain of hotels. Each one of these was a separate business, each with different services and priorities, but they all flowed out of the parent business.

What you need to do is keep an eye open for services and products that are related to what you are doing and see if there is an opportunity to provide a much-needed service or product. Start providing these new services, and see if that branch of the business takes off.

As you grow, divide those services into separate businesses. The beauty of this, of course, is that when it's time to exit a market, or when you tire of a company or feel it has achieved its potential, you will have the luxury of being able to pick and choose which ones to keep and which ones to sell.

To use an old saying, separating your businesses means that your eggs are not all in one basket even though they came from the same chicken. Creating different baskets multiplies your options, it spreads your risk, and it could lead you to even more opportunities that you never even considered before.

F O O T P R I N T   2 0

BUILD BASKETS
KRISTIAN FELDBORG, CO-FOUNDER POLICYCASTLE.COM, JUSTCOMPARE.CA, VESUVIOIS.COM

Biography

Kristian Feldborg has provided IT consultancy services to bank and insurance companies for the last 15 years. As an executive consultant, he has worked with retailers, investment banks and private equity companies looking to either acquire a banking license, buying or disposing of assets.

Kristian started Vesuvio three years ago, and the aim was to build a full-stack platform on which you could launch new insurance and banking propositions quickly. Vesuvio has since co-founded, and is providing the technology for, a UK digital home insurance broker www.policycastle.com. Vesuvio has also co-founded a price comparison site (www.justcompare.ca) for mortgages, credit cards and personal loans in Canada.

Are you an "all eggs in one basket" or a "many baskets" kind of entrepreneur.

I'm definitely a many baskets entrepreneur. You learn that quickly as an independent consultant. Especially if you work on large strategic executive advisory projects where there can be big gaps between the engagements. You have to always have a plan B. Over time, you get used to having more than one ball in the air and eventually it becomes the norm. As I moved into building a business, supplying software products and financial services, as opposed to consultancy, I brought with me the idea of building risk diversification into the model from the start.

Is having too many baskets a distraction?

Yes, of course it is a distraction, but in new businesses you get distracted all the time and it's a constant balancing act to make sure you allow yourself to get distracted by the right things. For me, the test is if the different activities move me closer to a common goal. If they don't, I have veered too far from the core. It is also important to make sure you schedule time for each task, so you don't frantically jump from one thing to another.

How did your business expand? How did that happen and how do you control it?

From a business perspective, being involved with a series of joint ventures means you gain access to an amount of resources you don't have yourself and most likely couldn't afford to recruit. If I had tried to run each project on my own, without partners, I would have instead hired product managers, who would be less experienced, less committed and much more reliant on my instruction and help. By engaging in multiple joint ventures at the same time, I am able to create synergies, fundraise faster, reduce my financial risk (because the eggs are not all in one basket), grow organically in different verticals and geographies and afford to build better quality solutions.

What are the great aspects of having many baskets as opposed to just one?

When you are building applications for financial services, what kills you are the lengthy sales cycles. If you have more than one horse in the race, you become less dependent on one particular deal landing this quarter, and it's not yourself who have to chase all the leads. So, in a way, having more baskets, actually allows me to focus more in the core development and proposition.

How many more baskets are you thinking of building?

Many. The model is definitely working for us and with two successful JVs under our belt, the aim is now to turn

Vesuvio into a real venture builder, working with more incredible founders, launching new fintech and InsurTech propositions.

ABOUT THE AUTHOR

PAUL OBERSCHNEIDER is living proof that the route to success is not a straight-line. Starting a business is not easy but anyone can do it if they have the right information. Paul's eventful journey took him from sleepy rural Illinois to life in the fast lane as a Wall Street trader, before losing almost everything to addictions and alcoholism and then starting from scratch.

Starting with no more than $400 in 1992, Paul grew a business that became a $200 million property powerhouse. In the process Paul discovered some basic rules for success that he shares in his book.

Paul's remarkable journey demonstrates how people who build successful businesses are driven by circumstances and then led by opportunity. Every entrepreneur possesses an essential set of skills, but what determines real success is how circumstances create the opportunities to bring these skills out, and then how willing they are to go with it and let things happen.

Success Leaves Footprints as Paul says, and Paul's new book will help you kick start your business adventure and guide the way.

Today, Paul is a seasoned entrepreneur and property financier. Since "retiring", aged 49, he has built a chain of fast food restaurants in London, and serves as a mentor for his Fast Track entrepreneur community and has written a best-selling business book called 'Why Sell Tacos in Africa that describes the journey of finding uncontested markets and building businesses.

Find more information on Paul and more about his programmes and courses at: www.pauloberschneider.com

PAUL'S FAST TRACK PROGRAMS

Kick Start (2-day programme)

Join Paul Oberschneider in a two-day crash course in Entrepreneurship and Disruptive marketing. Learn how Paul built a $200 million business starting with only $400 and was making $50,000 after 8 weeks. Discover the branding and marketing tools he used and how you can use the same tools to build your business. The two-day crash course is broken down into three success pillars'; Mindset, Money, and Scaling your business. It is run by Paul Oberschneider and will help you build a disruptive businesses and brand in 8 weeks. This two-day course offers entrepreneurs an indispensable kick-start programme to success.

Ignite (3-month programme)

This three-month programme comprises three full-day sessions over three months, with Paul going over the specific tools you need to grow your business, from cash flow management tools, funding tools, your business plan and deal memo writing and branding. Paul also invites relevant, top-level speakers from his 'little black book' to focus on topics that the class would otherwise never have access to. Being with an intimate group of other entrepreneurs makes the three-day programme invaluable for taking your business to the next level.

Accelerate (12-month programme)

It's easy to become lazy and complacent when your business hits a level of stability. This is a dangerous place to be. You may even forget some of your big dreams and think you can relax. Or maybe the next steps seem too big? There are the banks to deal with, funding and scaling issues to tackle, and then there's building a solid brand and identity. It may be overwhelming. But it doesn't need to be and this is the stage where with a bit more support and tools, you will start building your own empire. Accelerate addresses issues of this stage and helps you to focus on this important growth stage of your business. It's now or never. Don't get complacent—get cracking. Paul will also help you start thinking and planning for a successful exit. How to cash out those millions and retire. This is a programme where the hard topics of business are tackled and addressed. The power of this hand-picked group helps each other with Paul as the moderator and guide for the 12-month programme, is phenomenal.

Winner's Circle (private retreat)

A 10-day programme at Paul's private ranch is the place where brainstorming, questioning and testing ideas can produce amazing results and where planning the future takes place every day. Other topics may also include family issues, stress, dealing with difficult banking situations, problematic employees or workforces, taxes and succession planning as well as new business ideas and validation of those ideas. Paul's 10-day ranch experience is a spiritual business retreat for being in a safe and relaxing environment while taking the time to do some hard thinking and planning. Join the winners circle and make this an annual ritual—just like Paul does.

Contact us at admin@pauloberschneider.com for any queries or further info.